Mrs. Anna M. Faber
104 Del Mar Dr.
Jefferson City, MO 65109

R.M.
273

TO: Ann & Joe,

Thanks for your interest and support. I hope you both enjoy the book! There is so much that should not be forgotten. Best wishes.

Semper Fi,

Jerry Kuhn

"Once I started reading *Walk With Me* I found it extremely difficulty to put down. From the viewpoint of one who was there too, I found the book to be the most authentic and accurate accounting of the way it actually was that I have read. Lt. Colonel Kurth has truly captured the camaraderie, joys, suffering, fear and the conquering thereof, adrenaline rushes, and the ups and downs of surviving in a ground combat environment. Well done!"

Col. Skip Axtell, USMCR (Ret.)
Current President, E.A. Axtell, Jr. & Co.
Commercial-Industrial Realtors & Developers

"Lt. Colonel Kurth's novel invitation to participate in his Vietnam experience as a Marine officer engulfs the reader in the horrific, the bizarre and the humor experienced daily by Marines fighting their nation's battles and defending the Corps' honor 10,000 miles from home — just as Marines have done since 1775. Kurth's war experiences evoke empathy for the Marines who never lost a major military engagement and who lived the daily trials of jungle warfare, where they were both warrior and benevolent friend to villages caught in the devastating struggle between diverse economic and political systems. Kurth's candid story is an invaluable informative view of the transformation of eighteen year-old Marines to battled veterans. His story helps us understand why so many of our young men who went off to their nation's call to battle returned home forever changed by the experience that was Vietnam."

Judge Robert G. Ulrich, Missouri Court of Appeals
Colonel, USMCR (Ret)

"I must admit that I got caught up in Lt. Colonel Kurth's book. . . . One gets a strong sense of history, especially of Marine Corps history and tradition. While he deals with what was a controversial war and battle, I can't fault his account or judgment."

Alan Jones
Professor of History, Grinnell College(Ret.)

"Whether it be the battles in Vietnam, a corporate merger, or a daily task, it is clear that the person on the front line can best convey the experience. Lt. Colonel Kurth, without reserve, enlists *you* into his front line Vietnam experience. In this accounting he hits it hard, he hits it quickly and he keeps it moving. A most enlightening adventure. A must read."

Amy Noelker, Corporate Management, Sprint PCS

"It provides a view of the war that hasn't been seen enough."

Seymour M. Hersh
Former New York Times Reporter

"A story worth telling."

Congressman Ike Skelton

"While most of the strange sounding names of other varied locations of the American experience are long forgotten except by those who fought there — Khe Sanh remains frozen in memory ... The French defeat at Dien Bien Phu began the end of France's effort to hold on after World War II — were the Marines headed for the same end? Someone needed to tell the story of what happened at Khe Sanh and Lt. Colonel Kurth has done it. His book is a page turner from the beginning. Lt. Colonel Kurth's account catches the reality of the moment and freezes it in time."

Wm. Robert Pearman
Former Managing Editor, Kansas City Times
and Omaha World Herald

"I must say that I found ... your book to be such that I could not put it down once I started reading. The crisp, short chapters and variety of perspectives — from fun to horror, from uncertainty to audacity — reflected the multi-faceted way that life really was there and then. It was compelling to say the least."

Chaplain Ray W. Stubbe, USN
1st Battalion, 26th Marines

"I have served as a reviewer for many books in the past but none has so captivated and drawn me in as *Walk With Me*. This is clearly a book for thinking people who truly want to understand the emotion, tedium, humor and horror of war. In a war greatly criticized for the ineptness of American political leadership, this book reminds us that the American infantryman is still the world's finest and the character of their service remains undiminished.

Paul Thomson, Former President Blue River Community College;
Current President, Truman Heartland Community Foundation

WALK WITH ME:
A VIETNAM EXPERIENCE

By
Lt. Colonel Gerald F. Kurth, U.S.M.C. (Ret.)

A division of Squire Publishers, Inc.
4500 College Blvd.
Leawood, KS 66211
1/888/888-7696

Copyright 2000
Printed in the United States

ISBN: 1-58597-034-4

Library of Congress Catalog Card No. 00 133 117

A division of Squire Publishers, Inc.
4500 College Blvd.
Leawood, KS 66211
Phone: 1/888/888-7696

This book is dedicated to:

My son, Tracy Christopher Kurth

My wife, Marta L. Kurth

Chris saw me leave our family unit for 13 months on two separate occasions. Those childhood years were lost to us and I hope to make them up over the remainder of my life. It was his sincere interest and encouragement that caused me to relate these unique events. Once penned, he worked diligently to enter the text in the computer and complete the first edit. On numerous occasions, his suggestions and viewpoint aided greatly in developing the final copy.

Marta has been by my side for over forty years. Her unwavering support and love has truly been my strength.

A "G.I. Joe" drawing of me done by my son, Chris Kurth, when he was only eight years old while I was overseas on a 13-month unaccompanied tour on Okinawa (1973/74). His depiction of me is amazingly accurate, especially for such a young age — down to the nose, lips and entire profile. It came as a humorous surprise to learn that he visualized me with a perpetually heavy beard!

The drawings in Chapters 17, 26 and 33 were done as I wrote my book.

"Those who would understand the true nature of war must begin by understanding man's own nature, in its strength and in its weakness and in that fine balancing of good and evil, compassion amid brutality, hope amid ruins, and laughter in the middle of death, which gives man his unique capacity for survival."

Brig. Gen. S.L.A. Marshall

"As a human creature man is rational and emotional. But at the cutting-edge he is animal, framed in a struggle for existence. His and his opponent's lives are at stake, and in the clinch both are hurled back into the jungle age of history, in which survival values replace peacetime moralities. Everything that helps the soldier to survive is good; everything that does not is evil."

Maj. Gen. J.F.C. Fuller

"The human heart is the starting-point in all matters pertaining to the war."

Marshall Saxe

"They want war too methodical, too measured; I would make it brisk, bold, impetuous, perhaps sometimes even audacious."

Antoine Henri
Jomini

CONTENTS

PREFACE

NOT LONG AGO my wife and I were visiting our son, Chris, in Colorado. Chris and I had some time alone to talk while the women went to the mall. Like most American males, we weren't too keen on shopping so we opted out. In fact, once I even heard a report that men's blood pressure tends to go up while shopping. Chris was in the middle of writing a book on the martial arts and urged me to try my hand at writing as well. He specifically sighted a group of stories I shared with him about my 13-month tour of duty in Vietnam — from August 1967 to September 1968. This was ten years before I retired in 1978 from the Marine Corps as a Lt. Colonel — after serving a total of 20 years as a Marine infantry officer.

I had related some of these unique and bizarre experiences to Chris over the years and he has always found them fascinating. However, I never raved on and on about them or came near revealing all of these events. Based on the few that I did share, he felt it would make for interesting reading. It would let Americans, who did not participate in or do much reading about this conflict, get a feel for what really transpired and learn about other people's ordeals. Hopefully, then, readers would come too see this war in a different light. Most of these events didn't show up in the daily situation reports or on TV and selectively were buried.

Of course, I was delighted with his interest and told him that I would give it some serious thought. I was working in a new career, however, and free time was scarce. I joined the investment world in 1985 and have enjoyed helping people achieve their financial goals. I always have been goal oriented throughout my life and I've always felt that, if I can help other people to focus on their goals, I can add value to their lives. Thus, I am still working full time as Vice President-Investments at a major investment firm.

My first concern then about writing a book stemmed from the fact that it might detract from time spent in the investment business. Yet, since I didn't much care for the weekly TV offerings, I decided to devote that time to writing this book. I wasn't totally unfamiliar with writing, having written numerous articles for my Financial Focus and Money Trends columns in several suburban Kansas City newspapers. With this in mind, I made the plunge and began drafting an outline of my 13-month tour in Vietnam. Surprisingly, it was completed in a relatively short time and I was ready to share these experiences with friends.

As I said, the story outline unfolded smoothly and it gave me the requisite organization to tell this story. But, a nagging feeling suggested that something would be missing by just setting down a chronological series of events. I dwelled on this for days coming up with one concept title after another for the book, but nothing seemed right. Friends with whom I shared these titles leaned toward SNAFU (Situation Normal; All F—ked Up!). Although this title is somewhat appropriate, it seemed to me that this wasn't new and something was still missing.

Then one day, in a moment of relaxation gazing at Pike's Peak, it came to me. Instead of merely recounting each individual event, why not put you, the reader, right by my side "walking with me," like my alter ego or conscience. This way the reader could experience each event as it happened—sensing each reaction, judgment, horror or humorous episode as I originally had experienced it and giving you an opportunity to reflect on what your own actions might have been. These events did happen — and they happened exactly as I have recounted them! I had experienced many different reactions, but I was still a singular individual. My reactions affected many different people and helped shape several important events, but someone else might well have reacted differently.

That being the case, come along with me, you're personally invited! This second time will be better than the first, because I know you are with me and I'm not alone. You can get a firsthand glimpse of these events, become personally involved, and gain valuable experience and insight into the so-called "Vietnam conflict." I would like to believe that you will be more enlightened, knowledgeable and experienced after we finish our journey. So pack your gear, some extra socks, a raincoat, flack jacket, helmet, and good pair of boots — you are about to embark on one of the strangest experiences of your life. We will depart from Travis Air Force Base just outside San Francisco aboard a military leased 707 commercial airliner. Wherever you are coming from, I will meet you at the passenger terminal early in the morning of August 6, 1967.

*"The shadows of history fall heavy
on the shoulders of he who takes this journey."*

— *Sioux Indian saying*

INTRODUCTION: VIETNAM ASSIGNMENT

IT IS THE END of July 1967. I leave Kennedy International Airport in New York where I just put my wife and my only son, Chris, on an airliner bound for Morocco. We had been stationed there from 1963 to 1965—loving every minute of it and reluctant to leave. My wife needed somewhere to live with our new son, as we hastily had sold our Woodbridge, Virginia home. Since her mother and father had passed away, she decided to return to Morocco and rent a villa near the military installation, which had complete medical and shopping support. We would be halfway around the world from each other for 13 months—what a tremendous sacrifice for military men and their families to endure.

In Saint Louis, my parents, especially my mother, are concerned about my upcoming Vietnam tour and the inherent dangers. At this point, what would you tell your loved ones? In 1967 this war is not a popular conflict and that fact doesn't escape my parents. Since we are not defending the borders of the U.S. or making the world safe for democracy, my mother thinks I should refrain from participation by invoking the sole surviving son statute. It is true; I am the only son and child in our family and such a federal law exists. However, I quickly remind her that the U.S. Marine Corps is my career, already having served for eight years. I also tell her that I have trained long and am highly qualified, and feel I have a legal and moral responsibility to function as a leader to my fellow Marines. Besides, what future would I have in an elite military corps, if I elect to accept sole surviving status? I dismiss the concept immediately. You cannot find or opt for a way out either—you are walking with me!

It is encouraging to find you waiting patiently at the M.A.T.S. (Military Air Transport Service) terminal at Travis Air Force Base. You must be curious, nervous and excited about the upcoming adventure. I confess to experiencing these very same feelings. Since being commissioned in 1958, I have prepared myself for this eventuality and there is a sense of "I'm finally going to ply my trade and training and prove myself." Hence, let's get aboard!

When we depart Travis and reach cruising altitude, I look around at all the young men. It is a solemn occasion with many hiding their tear-streaked faces by peering out the airplane windows—getting a final glimpse of U.S. terra firma. It will be 13 months before these same faces will see their native land and families again. Some of those young men will never again see their families—returning instead sealed in a dark box. There is no doubt that everyone on the plane is calculating the odds. I start praying silently that I be granted a safe return to my loved ones.

As our aircraft glides over the expansive Pacific Ocean still several hours from landing in Vietnam, I recall how upset and disappointed I am with Lyndon Johnson's and Robert McNamara's arrogance and lack of political savvy—specifically for escalating the Vietnam Conflict into full-fledged U.S. involvement. Neither one knows much about history, especially Far Eastern and French history, having disregarded General Omar Bradley's warning to avoid involvement in a land war in Asia.

With plenty of time to reflect, my thoughts drift back to 1962 when I was a Marine Captain floating on a U.S. Navy ship just off the coast of Cuba. This was at the height of the Cuban missile crisis when we were poised to defend the U.S. against missiles launched from nearby Havana. We were putting teeth back into the Monroe Doctrine—a doctrine, you might recall, that unequivocally stated that no foreign power would be permitted to establish a military foothold in the Americas. Teddy Roosevelt, earlier in the century, gave the Germans an ultimatum demanding the removal of the German Navy from Venezuela within 72 hours. After a little more thought, he sent another message reducing the time frame to 48 hours! The Germans complied. Ironically, I was convinced the whole crisis theory was trumped up to test a young and inexperienced John F. Kennedy. I even tried to persuade my fellow officers that we would never go ashore and that Khruschev would back down. It was necessary to show our resolve and capability, since that's what was, indeed, being tested. Why did I set forth this premise and what was its validity?

I'm a prolific reader of history, especially Russian history. If anyone studies their history closely, they know that Russia has rarely been an aggressor—sweeping out from their borders to gobble up territory. Russia's interest in territory stems from repeated foreign invasions. Thus, they sought buffer territory. The long list of conquerors included the Monguls (they actually controlled Russia for 400 years), the Turks, the Swedes (Charles the XII), the French (Napolean), the Germans (twice—

U.S. Marine Corps 1st Lieutenants (left to right): Red Davis, John Salerno, York Feitel, Jerry Kurth, Doc Weinrie, USN, and Joe Schhimeneek on board a Navy APA troop transport passing through the Panama Canal in October 1962, bound for Cuba

Kaiser Wilhelm in 1916 and Adolph Hitler in 1941), and even the United States! Would not any nation become paranoid after so many invasions? It is also important to know Khruschev was privy to the fact that a U.S. Army Infantry Regiment, under the leadership of the English General Ironsides, fought the Red Army (Bolsheviks) south of Archangel in 1919. In addition, the U.S. Marine Corps seized the port of Vladisvostok and held it for several weeks during the same time frame. Yes, Virginia, we did invade Russia!

How does all this support my premise about Cuba? Quite simply, in a book written in 1957 entitled "Khruschev and the Russian Challenge," written by William Randolph Hearst, Jr., Bob Considine and Frank Conniff, Khruschev clearly showed his hand. Indeed, any State Department official assigned to study the Russian Premier should have been aware of this commentary from the book: "Khruschev seems to be honestly baffled by the way Hungary has 'stuck like a rat'—to use his own ugly phrase—in the throat of Western people. On his distorted scale of values, Soviet Russia was only acting the way a great power should in drastically eliminating a pressing menace." The foreign policy of Mother Russia is to establish buffer states, territory between them and invading armies. That way, when invasion comes, the invading army will have to traverse an expansive amount of terrain, and thereby lose its momentum. Of course, during the invaders' approach to Moscow, the Russian farmers would scorch the earth. It is a policy that has always triumphed. Further, "his study of what he calls 'Capitalist Nations' leads him to believe that they would act similarly if confronted with a comparable challenge....We will hazard to guess that Khruschev expects the U.S. to take just the same steps should it ever be confronted with a dangerous revolt in its own front yard. He hardly anticipates that we will sit idly by, for instance, should a Communist government take over Panama. Nor does Khruschev, with his pragmatic view of affairs, expect we would allow Cuba to become a Communist satellite before our very eyes....He still has enough respect for us as a great power, however, to believe that we will act in our own best interests should a real crisis arise....But, if we were ever to stand back while the Panama Canal slipped into hostile hands, or while a Communist puppet government began to build rocket bases in Cuba, Khruschev would first of all be very much surprised; then he would draw the conclusion that America's day as a great power was over. He would, we firmly believe, become a dangerous exponent of brinkmanship from that moment on, and nuclear war would be much more of a possibility than it is now, when Khruschev still believes we will not shy from taking all measures, included unpopular ones, to safeguard our security" (pp. 208-209). These conclusions were postulated during Mr. Khruschev's visit to the U.S., arriving at Andrews Air Force Base on September 15, 1959.

The tragic events in Cuba, culminating in the fiasco at the Bay of Pigs, when a timid and uncertain president, listening to ridiculous advise from inexperienced State Department officials, failed to support the Cuban Brigade of Freedom fighters caused Mr. Khruschev to reevaluate our resolve "to safeguard our security." Hence, the Cuban Missile Crisis three years later. You need to understand—the Soviets (Mother Russia) were prepared to fight in Hungary and Czechoslovakia, buffer zones, but not in Cuba!

However, I know from a synopsis of all that I read on Vietnam, that the North Vietnamese and Viet Cong would fight us every inch of the way. We would win only if we launch a massive invasion (such as Inchon in 1950) to shut down the North or if the people learn to support an effective and honest South Vietnamese regime. The West never did comprehend how much the Vietnamese people want to reunite and become one nation again. If President Lincoln could pull it off, so could Ho Chi Minh—and Ho Chi Minh had studied in Europe and knew U.S. history. The key question is whether or not the U.S. will commit sufficient forces to actually win the war. Also of great importance—will the military be allowed to conduct the war or will U.S. politicians intervene and condemn us to defeat, as they did in the Bay of Pigs?

In that state, one hour from landing in the middle of the so-called "Vietnam Conflict," I wonder what is in store for us and what course of action our leaders will take? The next 13 months clearly will answer these questions; and, sadly, humorously, and honestly tell you about the Vietnam War.

Someone on the starboard side of the plane yells, "There's land." We all strain to get our first glimpse of war-torn Vietnam. In my case, it will be my first sight of Asian territory since my travels with the 7th Fleet as a 1st Lieutenant in 1960-61. It's also probably your first glimpse of the Far East. What I see next makes my heart race. Columns of black smoke are rising high into the afternoon sky from fires burning adjacent to the runway. I wonder what is going through your mind—is the war starting for us so soon? Well, friends, welcome to Vietnam—with all its chaos, uncertainty and suffering! Maybe Mom was right!

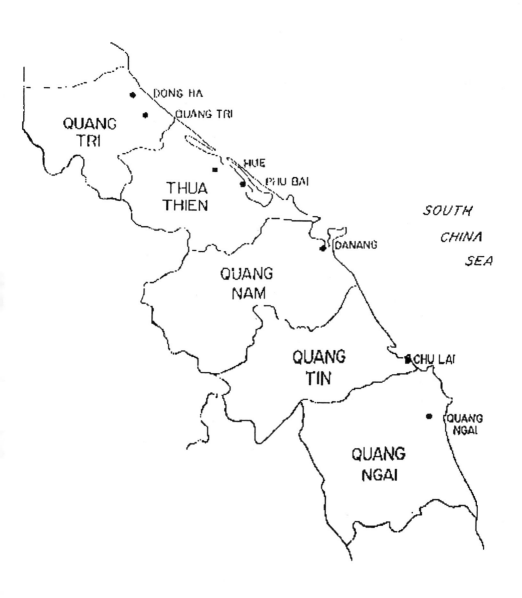

DONG HA

QUANG TRI

QUANG TRI

HUE

THUA THIEN

PHU BAI

SOUTH

CHINA

SEA

DANANG

QUANG NAM

QUANG TIN

CHU LAI

QUANG NGAI

QUANG NGAI

I Corps

Tactical Zone

Part I

HUE / PHU BAI TAOR

HUE / PHU BAI TAOR

ONCE ON THE GROUND we learn that we just landed at Phu Bai, Vietnam. The fires aligning the airfield are the remains of aircraft that were damaged or destroyed in a Viet Cong mortar attack the previous night. The transportation from the airfield takes us to the Headquarters area for the 3rd Marine Division in the Thua Thien Province of the I-Corps Tactical Area just below the DMZ (Demilitarized Zone). The DMZ runs between North and South Vietnam and signifies the civil war now in progress. Once at Headquarters, we are taken to officer billeting to deposit our baggage and to report to the G-1 (General Staff Administration) for our assignments. I had been feeling that since I am a very senior Captain, having just completed Amphibious Warfare School in Quantico, Virginia, that I would be assigned a staff billet, as opposed to infantry Company Commander. It doesn't take long to get an assignment — Assistant S-3 Operations Officer of the 2nd Battalion, 26th Marine Regiment. This battalion is assigned responsibility for tactical control of the Hue/Phu Bai TAOR. TAOR stands for Tactical Area of Responsibility (see map). The TAOR stretches 26 miles along the infamous Route 1 — the so-called "Street Without Joy," made famous by Bernard Fall.

I really like this assignment because it is a key staff job that deals with the tactical day-to-day deployment of the battalion's four rifle companies (and also the Headquarters Company). Only two weeks into my tour, I assume the sole duties as the new Operations Officer of the battalion, replacing a Major who is reassigned. You will be at my right

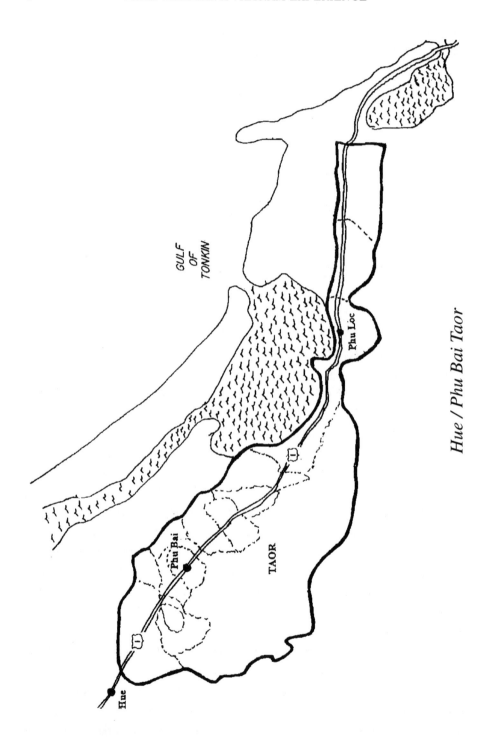

GULF OF TONKIN

Phu Loc

Phu Bai

TAOR

Hue

Hue / Phu Bai Taor

hand for the next 12-1/2 months as we deploy and fight a Marine infantry unit of approximately 1,200 U.S. Marines. Also, keep in mind that a majority of these Marines are between the ages of 18 and 20 years — an awesome responsibility, don't you think? Unable to vote or drink legally in their homeland, these young men are committed 8,000 miles from home at the whim of President Johnson. The reason given by the politicians is to stop the so-called "domino effect" — that is, the incremental fall of South East Asian countries to Communist governments.

The command bunker for the battalion at the Phu Bai Combat Base is located several feet underground near the middle of the compound. The overall size of the bunker is about 25 by 25 feet. It is the home of the COC (Combat Operations Center) — the location from which we communicate with all of our various companies throughout the 26-mile Hue/ Phu Bai TAOR — E, F, G, H, HQ CO, Division G-3, Artillery, Marine Aircraft, and the Vietnam District Leaders. In this environment, you will spend late evening hours with me waiting patiently until the need for swift reaction arrives — with no mistakes allowed.

I find it easy to work for Battalion Commander, Lieutenant Colonel Duncan Chaplin. He allows me to do the planning and coordination to fight the battalion — giving final approval on each idea or plan. However, he does not share the bunker with me and only appears when the proverbial "shit hits the fan"! His quarters are in the HQ Company, 2nd Battalion, 26th Marines office and billeting area in the middle of the combat base. Wooden huts house all the officers and personnel of our battalion. However, I have erected a CP (Command Post) tent near the entrance of our COC bunker so I (we) can sleep in close proximity to the command center and respond quickly to any emergency. The only piece of furniture is a canvas sleeping cot. I have a blanket for evenings, but I always make sure it doesn't touch the ground since rats will run up the blanket and over me (us). I can hear them scurrying around in the dark. Curious about how many there are, I smooth out the dirt floor and then view the tracks in the morning. It is not good news.

Upon my assuming the duties as operations officer, our current deployment of the units has one company in the southern area of the TAOR, another about midpoint in the TAOR, and the other two in and around

3rd MARINE DIVISION

5th MARINE DIVISION

2nd Battalion, 26th Marines was activated for Vietnam and placed under operational control of the 3rd Marine Division. Originally, it was part of the 5th Marine Division in World War II (commissioned on November 11, 1943 and disbanded in December 1945).

Phu Bai Combat Base Main Gate

the Phu Bai base itself. The mortar attack against the Phu Bai airstrip means the Viet Cong or NVA are relatively close to the base. If we are going to prevent such further attacks, we will have to develop more successful tactics.

This is my first major tactical decision. I divide the TAOR into three separate areas, placing a 150-man rifle company in each. The fourth company and the HQ Company are retained inside the Phu Bai base, but patrol just beyond mortar range (approximately a mile around the base). In all four areas, the companies send out platoon-sized patrols during the day, preselecting an ambush sight for overnight and then moving unseen into that area under the cover of darkness. The ambush sights are generally along known trails or avenues of approach and egress to villages. By so doing, the VC (Viet Cong) and/or NVA (North Vietnamese Army) will see us active during the day, probably not engage us in a firefight (as we can outgun them), and then be uncertain where we are during the nights when we like to move. Therefore, on any given night the entire battalion has anywhere from 12 to 16 major ambush sights throughout the TAOR. Three of these ambush sights are kept within a mile radius of the Phu Bai Combat Base. Also, we usually keep one rifle platoon in stand-down condition aboard the base to catch up on rest, laundry, hygiene (cold showers) and a good "drying out." The four rifle companies are rotated periodically so each group will have a stint operating out of the base.

The toughest part of this tactic is driving up and down Route 1 to systematically visit and supervise the units in the field. For this task, I utilize two jeeps that carry four people each. These two jeeps consist of my Radio Operator, Forward Air Controller (they direct and vector in Marine aircraft strikes in support of the ground forces), two drivers (also acting as back-up security), an Artillery Forward Observer (they call in artillery support), and two security guards.

This time around we will drop off one of the guards and add you to the entourage. We will drive several miles through contested territory, spend one night with a Company Commander, and then head back to Phu Bai, hoping that we are never ambushed! How comfortable do you feel now? We're just getting started.

Chapter 1

WHEN THE HELL CAN WE SHOOT?

AFTER MY FIRST TWO WEEKS as the Operations Officer, the four companies are deployed. I'm thoroughly ensconced in the COC and we've commenced a very aggressive patrol program throughout the TAOR. I must confess that I feel quite proud being assigned the Operations Officer as a 31-year-old Captain, since it is a Major's billet. As a career officer, highly visible and responsible jobs are essential for future promotion. I feel fully qualified and quite confident, especially having just completed the six-month Amphibious Warfare School program at Quantico, Virginia. It gave me the requisite training to function effectively as an Operations Officer and Battalion Commander. Confidence developed over the years by achievement and overcoming vicissitudes is now my trump card.

The COC is my very own "Corporate HQ" to run and I now feel prepared for any contingency or engagement. Ironically, nothing significant or even interesting has developed these first days of September — no enemy engagements — not even a sighting. I am frustrated and want my first action (or test). One never really knows what his reaction will be when placed in an unfolding operational situation and actual combat. I need action and validation of my own skills and psychological reaction. I sense that the other junior officers and senior staff NCO's (Non-Commissioned Officers) are measuring me and are curious about how I will orchestrate the show — hoping for professional and decisive leadership. Already I'm getting queries from the officers in the COC

Lt. Colonel Duncan Chaplin, CO, 2/26, and Lt. Colonel Banks, 3rd Marine Division Staff, visit me in the Phu Bai COC bunker. The map of the Phu Bai Combat Base is on left, and the Hue / Phu Bai TAOR, with unit deployments, is on right.

such as, "Captain, do you think the Viet Cong will mortar the base anytime soon?" or "Boy, the size of this monstrous TAOR concerns me!" I answer all questions and comments with absolute confidence, truth and professionalism. I perceive that they believe me.

It is mid-afternoon the second week of September when the radio finally comes alive with an excited situation report from one of the patrol leaders in the field. The patrol has spotted a large Viet Cong unit packing weapons, including 82 mm mortars, coming out of the western hills moving east to northeast. The patrol leader seeks permission to open fire with mortars and calls for artillery support to engage the enemy. We finally are presented with a lucrative target.

However, in the COC, a directive entitled the "Rules of Engagement" spells out the procedures we need to follow prior to opening fire. All fire support personnel have been briefed and have a hard copy of the rules posted near the radio for reference. The rules deal with the many Vietnamese political "districts" that are present in our vast TAOR and they must be applied carefully. In populated, built-up areas, all fire missions on enemy forces within the boundaries of these districts need clearance from that particular Vietnamese District Chief. This is not the case in rural or uninhabited areas. We, of course, need to consider consequences to civilians in populated village areas. I have no problem with that concept.

Before we fire a shot, the Viet Cong unit crosses a district boundary. I immediately contact the District Chief's headquarters and wait as they try to locate him. The delay is agonizingly prolonged and our frustration mounts. When he finally gives his permission, the lead elements of the patrol have crossed into another district! The initial opportunity to engage the enemy is lost — the second one as well!

We hastily shift radio frequency to the adjacent district and summon that District Chief. He too is predisposed and delays coming up on the radio; however, his representative finally does. After we feed him the map coordinates, we again locate the enemy, but find that they have moved. We quickly recalculate, update the map coordinates, and inform the district of their exact location. Finally — clearance to fire! Yet, luck evades us!

They have passed out of the second district. We need further clearance to fire with yet another political entity! Disappointment and disgust escalate to controlled rage. We work feverishly to get a final shot at this prime enemy target, but we have to clear the action with yet another political entity. It never works out. I still don't have the authority to fire a single round. They could turn right around and we will have to go through same agonizing process.

You witness it — no clearance, no engagement, and very poor communication. We have lost the opportunity! This indeed is going to be a very different, absurd kind of war — replete with political restrictions and curious undertones. How in the hell can we win if we can't engage? The last communication from the Marine Lieutenant, calling from deep within the field, punctuates the silence in the COC bunker and speaks for us all: "When the hell can we shoot?"

Chapter 2

BACK TO THE RIFLE RANGE

BY THE END OF SEPTEMBER 1967, our patrol tactics appear to be quite successful on several occasions as we engage the enemy moving about at night. During each firefight, I communicate with the Patrol Leader on the radio receiving situation reports and any other information I can gather. Since it is nighttime, the final results cannot be tallied until daybreak. Upon first light, the Patrol Leaders will assess the results and give us the final SITREP (situation report).

I begin to realize that, although there are numerous contacts with the enemy, there are very questionable results. One hates to deal with cold realities; but, nevertheless, "results" are measured in terms of dead enemy soldiers — the so-called "body count." I'm sure you find this a bit unsettling, but it's the brutal reality of war. The body count is extremely important in 1967, as President Johnson wants hard figures to counteract increasing protest marches. The most important figure is the total number of dead enemy soldiers, although these body counts often are padded. The administration needs this figure to quantify the progress of this questionable war.

The next time I receive substandard counts, I decide that I need to visit each enemy engagement sight personally to ascertain just what is causing such poor results. It doesn't take long to figure out. After just two visits, debriefing each Marine and Patrol Leader, I uncover the problem — poor marksmanship!

Fortunately, I had attended an advanced marksmanship course at Camp Pendleton, California in 1961 taught by some of the best marksmen in the history of the Corps. They taught me so well that in 1962 I was Captain of the 5th Marine Regiment Rifle and Pistol Team — a team that competed in the Marine Corps Western Division Matches preparatory to service-wide competition at Camp Perry, Ohio. I had the good fortune of watching Gunny Sergeant Pieterfort and Captain McMillan compete on the rifle range at Chappo Flats. I saw McMillan win a case of beer from Pieterfort when he "cleaned the course" one day (never missing the white bulls-eye from 200 yards while standing, 300 yards while sitting and kneeling, and 600 yards from the prone position). He beat Pieterfort by one point — only one point! If you check the records at Camp Perry you will see that Gunny Pieterfort even won the National Rifle Competition one year.

Our unsatisfactory shooting centers on the average Marine's poor knowledge of marksmanship. At this time, these Marines simply are being trained too fast. They have limited experience with setting the sights on the new M-16 rifle, which gradually replaced the older M-14, and they actually are shooting over the enemy's heads. It probably scares the crap out of "Charlie" (our name for the Viet Cong), but we sure aren't going to win the war unless some changes are made. Now that I've determined the problem, what's your suggestion?

How about back to "Rifle Range 101." You bet — but where, how and when? Do you stop the war; do we even have time to solve the problem? No more questions — we need a fast solution. The best answer is to go somewhere in close proximity to the combat base and find appropriate grounds for a makeshift rifle range. All we have to do is measure off some selected distances (I choose 25, 50, 100 and 200 yards), put up some targets, and hold on-the-spot marksmanship training.

Actually, we find a great location on an adjacent engineering base. There we set up numerous wooden silhouette practice targets. Next, we rotate one platoon at a time out of combat for impromptu marksmanship training. We don't have "target-pullers" in the target pit, as we had in the states, so we merely determine the results with binoculars to see if they are hitting the silhouettes. I select several NCO marksmanship-training instructors from our experienced shooters and do some training myself.

The NCO's are magnificent at this task. Our motor transport support also performs fantastically, as they respond promptly, professionally and enthusiastically to our needs. They move unit after unit onto the base for marksmanship training and then head back down Route 1 for redeployment. God, I love the Corps and its "esprit"! Go to just one Sunset Marine Parade at the 8th and I Street Marine Barracks in Washington, D.C. on any Friday night during the summer and you'll see what I'm talking about.

There are some real concomitant benefits from all of this activity. First, it demonstrates concern and willingness on our part to give our men the requisite training to complete their task (and keep them alive). Second, it is a unique experience for the units, which definitely need a change of pace. Rather than walking around the wilderness laying ambushes with such questionable results, the men actually get feedback for their hard work and training. Third, I suspect that Charlie really doesn't understand all the troop movement — the Cong probably thinks we are being reinforced.

The results are remarkable. And here I suspect we both have ambivalent feelings, since the "results" are more dead humans —

Captain Cliff Griesen visits me outside the Combat Operations Center (COC) at Phu Bai Combat Base. We had served together in Morocco in 1964/1965.

something a rational human being shouldn't be happy about. But, in a war, the issue simply boils down to "us" verses "them." As professional soldiers we have a job to do. Still, killing can't help but weigh heavily on your sensibilities. Although you probably agree with my actions so far — just wait. Your morality is just starting to be challenged.

Chapter 3

GET THOSE TRUCKS MOVING

AS OCTOBER DAWNS, we decide to move one of our rifle companies to the southern extremities of the Hue/Phu Bai TAOR. This area centers on a town called Phu Loc. The rifle company moves out of Phu Bai Combat Base on several 6 x 6 2-1/2-ton trucks (the workhorse of motor transportation) and heads down the "Street Without Joy" (aka Route 1) toward its destination.

I elect to travel along with the column in our two jeeps, as I have yet to conduct a physical reconnaissance of that area. It will also be a good opportunity for you to see more of Vietnam. It is a long trip and it dawns on me what a huge chunk of territory we are assigned! Highway 1 is a paved two-lane ribbon of concrete extending north and south along the entire East Coast of Vietnam. It is 900 plus miles from Hanoi to Saigon. One immediate concern is the 26-mile stretch of the highway running from Hue City in the north to the Lang Ko bridge in the south.

We already have become quite familiar with this extremely important line of communication. On several occasions, we conduct low-level helicopter reconnaissance flights along key sections of the route. Those are totally "hairy" and spine-tingling experiences. Marine air provides the Huey helicopter. The pilots are true professionals and fearless in their performance. We take off from the Hue/Phu Bai military airfield and head for the section of road I wish to reconnoiter. Upon reaching our starting point, the pilot drops the Huey to only 50 feet (yes, 50 feet)

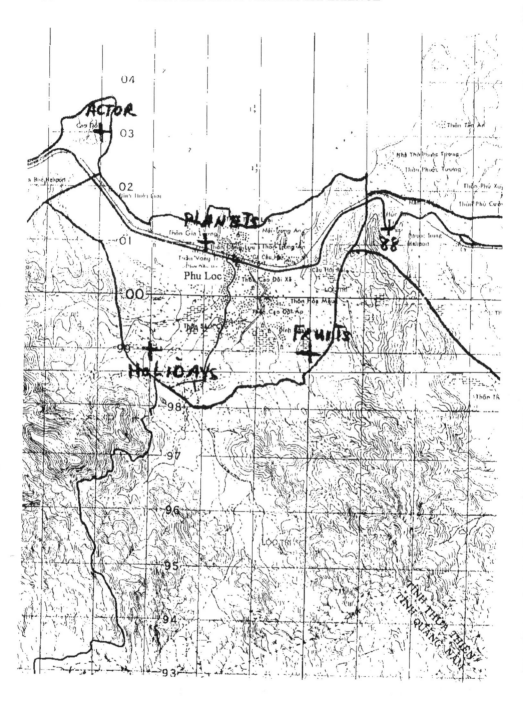

Phu Loc Village

above the roadway. He then dips down the nose and raises the rear rotor. We find ourselves at about a 15° slant. With this configuration, we now look directly down at the concrete! If I were not buckled into the seat next to the pilot, I would fall forward through the front glass window. You are strapped in the seat right behind me, and, if your safety belt comes loose, you will tumble over my seat and follow me out the window. I doubt whether you have experienced a more death-defying ride at any amusement park. Vehicles, people, trees, animals, telephone poles, power lines and birds whiz by us on the right, left and below on the ground as we propel down the Street Without Joy. Hell—there is little joy or fun in any of these endeavors! I try to concentrate on the task at hand, but my stomach somersaults. I hope you have a high tolerance for motion. These crazy "sky jockeys" like to give us "grunt infantry officers" a ride for our money, but I don't want to give him the satisfaction of knowing he has shaken me up. It will sure feel good again when my feet hit solid earth. This serves as revalidation for my decision to decline flight school while checking in the Officer Candidate Course at Quantico, Virginia.

As we arrive at Phu Loc, we pull off Route 1 to stop on the side of the road. One by one the trucks disgorge their troops. Just as we finish unloading, an explosion erupts, then another, then another. Mortar rounds rain down on us. We obviously are under enemy fire. I race over to the Marine officer-in-charge of the truck convoy, a Lieutenant, and yell at him to move the damn trucks!

Immediately, the trucks clear out and speed home north. The newly arrived Marines quickly disburse, and you and I hit the deck. I feel the ground tremble each time a mortar round explodes — the further away, the lighter the shudder; the closer they come, the more I wince and hug the earth. When some debris falls on the back of my legs, I know it is too damn close. I can't help imagining a mortar round already in the air heading silently in my direction and ending my life in an instant. The agonizing waiting, the ability to do nothing, and the random nature of the explosions sicken me. What a rude welcome to the southern confines of our Tactical Area of Responsibility (TAOR). Charlie obviously is in the vicinity!

The shelling doesn't last long, but it is my first time under enemy fire and most likely a new "experience" for you as well. At this moment the war seems totally realistic and the danger of our involvement finally sinks in. No one is killed or even wounded in the attack, but it gets everyone's attention. I end up spending the night near Phu Loc with the Company Commander since there is not enough daylight left to traverse Route 1.

After a delicious breakfast of military C-rations, one last map coordination check, and a pep talk, we climb into our jeeps for the return trip to Phu Bai. I would be lying if I didn't confess that I was worried about driving 20 miles through such hostile territory. Unfortunately, these solo trips will become commonplace in the months ahead. I wonder if I will ever be captured — worse probably than being killed in action. It is truly a crapshoot every time we travel on these dangerous roads.

(NOTE: Now, let's fast forward 21 years to Kansas City — it's 1988. I have retired from the Corps in 1978 and am working as an Investment Representative with a New York Stock Exchange firm in an office located in the Kansas City suburbs. One day, this gentleman walks into my office to discuss investments. From the "get go," I think he looks familiar, but it is merely a passing thought. After awhile, he asks me if we have met before because I also look familiar to him. Nothing checks out and I begin asking numerous questions about his background and financial situation. Soon, he interrupts to ask if I had ever served with the U.S. Marine Corps. When I confirm that I had, he blurts out, "I know who you are! I was a Motor Transport Officer in Vietnam and you were the hard-ass Major who told me to 'move those damn trucks' near Phu Loc in 1967." Now I remember him! We both laugh and are taken aback by what a small world it really is. Happily, our association is reestablished under much more peaceful and familiar surroundings.)

Chapter 4

BYE, BYE M-14

THE STANDARD FIREARM carried by a Marine Major in a combat situation is a Colt .45 handgun. If you aren't familiar with the .45, please recall that while we were together on the rifle range, I held a class for you on pistol shooting. You also have become quite proficient with the M-14 rifle, which is the rifle I still carry on our countrywide motor movements. You learn to shoot quickly scoring with the proficiency of a Marksman. You even comment that you feel reasonably at home with this weapon.

Surprisingly, my wife actually earned the Sharpshooter rating with the .45 pistol her first time on the target range — a skill she reminds me of on numerous occasions during our marriage. I was quite impressed by her achievement, as some Marines work hard to attain this expertise.

In tough times, I gain confidence by picturing myself with the incredible shooting ability of Jimmy Stewart in "Winchester 73." This role-playing approach works. A high standard of marksmanship makes us feel secure.

The principal reason we need this degree of proficiency stems from the fact that we will be spending a lot of time en route. When you're in hostile territory, you better be able to engage the enemy effectively at 300 yards or more. The idea, of course, is to get them first, kill them, keep them at bay, or, at least, impress them. This way they might think twice before engaging us again.

Our units now carry the new M-16 rifle, which replaced the M-14, but I want nothing to do with these toy-like M-16's. We even joke that they are made by the Mattel toy corporation. It is an awkward weapon — too tinny and the cartridges sometimes jam in the chamber. This cartridge jam effectively disables the weapon, making it impossible to fire. We all feel this new rifle is absurd. We even wonder if they had tested it before giving it to us. Earlier this May several Marines lost their lives near Khe Sanh when their weapons jammed. Some were killed on the side of Hill 661 as they were attempting to clear their damn M-16's.

The M-16 muzzle velocity is extremely fast, which is okay, except their bullets are too small — they simply shatter on impact with foliage. Because of this high-tense velocity, even small tree limbs can affect the bullets. Besides, why should we change rifles, we already know how to use the M-14. We also need the long-range proficiency that our M-14's provided! This new weapon is simply a lousy trade-off — no matter how you look at it.

It isn't long after conversion to the new M-16's when I receive a call from the 3rd Marine Division G-3 Officer (the HQ Operations Officer— my counterpart two levels up the chain of command). I drive over to see this Colonel and decide to bring you along so that you could see the Division Headquarters. Not only will this be a good learning experience for you, but I also can introduce you to the G-1 (Director of Administration and Personnel), the G-2 (Director of Military Intelligence), G-4 (Director of Logistics & Supply), and the G-5 (Director of Civil Affairs) officers. All of these men provide support to us down the chain of command. We subsequently report to the Colonel's office, whereupon, without niceties, he tells me to turn in my M-14 and draw the new M-16!

Your response is the same as mine — to wit: "Colonel, I run down Route 1 several times a week visiting our subordinate units throughout our TAOR and I want that M-14 proficiency — we could get ambushed at any time and the M-14 has a better range." He pays little heed and simply mentions the trade-off again. I can't contain myself and feel this issue is important enough to defend, "Colonel, with all due respect, it's not you or any of the Division Staff running that road and I really feel safer with the M-14."

I guess that doesn't go over too well because I barely finish before he blurts out, "That's a direct order — our conversation is terminated." Marines do not salute indoors, so I say, "Aye, aye, Sir," wheel around, and leave promptly. What do you think about this little exchange? You are part of an elite combat Corps and you don't want to screw up your future career. Indeed, an order is an order, and, if it's a legal order, it must be followed. Unfortunately, it is legal.

We turn in the M-14's and draw that lousy "piece of work," as we call it. Some character sold the U.S. Army a bill of goods. Ironically, the Marine Corps actually wanted a different weapon, which I saw fired at a demonstration in Quantico, Virginia. It certainly was better than the Army's "Toys 'R Us" weapon that they were foisting upon us. The Marine Corps field-tested the M-16 in Vietnam utilizing B Company, 1st Battalion, 3rd Marines, from August to November 1965. After this test the Corps proclaimed it "unsatisfactory." The Defense Department bureaucrats — with their vast weapons experience — would not allow two different weapons systems for the Army and the Marines. In fact, there

Major Kurth outside COC bunker at Phu Bai with jeep driver

is some evidence that the Air Force initially sought to employ the M-16 rifle for their sentry and guard personnel. The cartridges they proposed to use were packed with extruded powder. The Army felt they also could utilize the weapon, but would substitute ball powder. The ball powder was too explosive for the cartridge configuration, thereby generating a violent explosion that caused the cartridge to jam in the chamber. Whether this is all totally true or not isn't the important aspect. The important reality is that the cartridge does jam and the weapon's testing ignored. How could such an innovative, creative and quality industrial/military complex provide such a poor weapon to its fighting men — thereby endangering their lives? You don't suppose money had anything to do with it, do you? The provision of two different weapons simply was not cost effective. I sure would like to talk to the men who made this decision. The Viet Cong's AK-47 is a far superior weapon. It can withstand rain, mud and dirt far better than the M-16. Of course, we have to take the new M-16's. We even do some target practice with them. Yet, we never feel as comfortable or safe as we did with our more reliable M-14's. You probably are asking yourself, "How can we live with such autocratic leadership?"

Chapter 5

IT'LL BREAK YOUR HEART

IT IS NOW the middle of October 1967, and we have received intelligence reports about a couple of villages that seem sympathetic to Charlie. This means that these villages could be caching weapons and food for the Viet Cong's ongoing operations in our TAOR. The Battalion Commander and I discuss it, and he asks me what I think we should do. My recommendation is that I join our rifle company operating in that vicinity and conduct a search and clear operation. Not only will we pull together all the platoons of that company, but I also will bring down a reinforcement platoon from Phu Bai Base. We ride in the workhorse 6 x 6 trucks that we typically use for this sort of large troop movement. Once we arrive, I then will have a formidable infantry unit to conduct the operation and deal with any combat situation that arises.

We meet near the bridge at Thon An Nong where I take command of the newly reinforced company. Finally, this is your chance to see a larger unit in operation. We now have a force of almost 250 hardened United States Marines. They firmly believe that they can't lose and I know damn well we can't lose either! If you're still not that confident, you soon will be.

As we move, we fan out to the west of the village. A veteran Marine unit in full combat gear, weapons at the ready, negotiates its way across rice paddies and begins closing in. The sky is virtually cloudless, which is always a blessing to a Marine ground unit since close air support is

The edge of the Vietnamese village as we moved through on our search and clear mission.

assured. It is an impressive sight. I have command communications next to me with the capability of vectoring in a Marine F-4 Phantom jet fighter, calling for 105mm and 155mm artillery support, as well as calling for our own 81mm mortars. I suppose that, like Lieutenant Calley at My Lai, we are poised to reek some real havoc. The fire support available is indescribable. We can turn a hillside into a facsimile of the face of the moon! We slowly close our trap and the tension is running high. If we unleash all of our destructive power, we would make My Lai look relatively tame. Our command group is moving slightly behind the lead Marine elements on the road winding into the village. Radio antennas stick up everywhere. We try to stay disbursed somewhat so we aren't such a prime and vulnerable target. However, the radio operators need to be fairly close so we can send directions and orders when necessary. The road is dusty and the wind is picking up. We can begin to smell some of the cooking odors drifting in our direction.

There is no enemy fire from the village, which actually looks rather large to be called a "village." Several inhabitants hurry about the streets, most with concerned looks that you will come to expect. Frankly, I am waiting for all hell to break loose and I pray to God that nothing terrible happens. I feel this way for several reasons. First, there would be many innocent people involved, including many small children. Second, I don't want to be responsible for losing some of the young 17- to 20-year-old Marines under my command — that inevitably with odds will come at some point in time! After a while, we enter the center of the village. Our command element is getting situation reports from the four Platoon Commanders spread through the area. To our surprise, nothing has happened. As I look over at you, I read relief on your face. At this moment, a small entourage — a total of five men plus an elderly man — makes its way to our location. As they come closer, I surmise that they are members of the village council. This 80-year-old man — he might be even older than that — stops directly in front of me. He must have surmised that I am in charge because of all the damn radios surrounding me, or maybe it is because of my age or size. This is a little disconcerting, as it means that I would be the primary target had there been enemy fire! Every one of the Vietnamese stands considerably smaller than our Marines. They are dressed in the traditional loose-fitting Vietnamese clothes — each donning a conical straw hat that serves to fend off the sun and rain — very practical. Their faces are extremely solemn and wrinkled. By the looks of their teeth, it appears that dentists are nonexistent in their village society. The chief begins speaking to me in a distinctively passionate voice. Since we always have a Vietnamese interpreter with us, I ask him to translate. The old man is in fact making a fervent plea not to confiscate some of the foodstuff that our troops have uncovered. Tears run down his weathered face as he begs us to be merciful!

As he speaks and the interpreter relates it to me in English, my eyes begin to scan the village. I notice the straw-thatched roofs on each of the buildings, the people gathered around several fires cooking food, and children anxiously peering out from behind the perceived security of the adults. Like everywhere else in the world, the young children are cute, wide-eyed, energetic and innocent. Normally, the children gather around our Marines as they near a village, since the men can't resist passing out chocolates or other treats. It always amazes and pleases me how compassionate our men are to the local population. There are no paved streets, fire hydrants, storefronts, streetlights or telephone booths here. The

Some of the Vietnamese ignore our operations and continue about their daily business.

average American simply cannot relate to their base existence and lack of amenities. And, yet, it is peaceful and somehow I feel a sense of community exists. The oriental family values always have impressed me, whether I see it in Vietnam, Okinawa, Japan, China, or in many Asian-American families.

The same village chief also has to deal with Viet Cong leaders and units that move through his village demanding cooperation. There are many instances where the VC threatened and even killed South Vietnam villagers to elicit support. The brutality to their southern countrymen oftentimes is unbelievable.

Prior to our arrival in the TAOR, an especially brutal incident took place. The VC cut off the heads of the village chief, his wife and two children because the village head refused collaboration with them. Their rotting heads mounted on poles outside the village stood as a warning to all others. The American press gives little coverage to VC/NVA atrocities.

I am pretty choked up by this and am fighting back emotions of my own. You must be deeply touched as well. The principal thought that keeps racing through my mind is how would I feel if a Russian or Chinese military unit showed up with all these weapons and threatened Stowe,

VT; Chilton, WI; Lee's Summit, MO; Holly Springs, MS; San Clemente, CA — or any small town in the United States, for that matter. I actually am embarrassed so I order a prompt withdrawal from the village. I sense that the Marines who witness this exchange also are glad we are leaving. My parting thought ironically is of President Johnson — I sure wish that he had witnessed this incident. After this, I never again view our presence in Vietnam in a good light. It is also the first crack in my Marine career plan. I imagine that by now you want out and we've only been here two months.

Chapter 6

34–36–38 / A–B–C OR D

LET'S GET BACK to our patrol activities because they are always on-going, aggressive and effective. I am certain that our marksmanship training was beneficial — it not only has engendered greater confidence, but it also has brought positive results in battle. We are about to collect the first big dividends.

The nights are typically monotonous as we stand vigilant in our Phu Bai COC bunker. We have delineated the patrol activity and ambush sites on the situation map. As the time passes in silence, we wait patiently in the underground bunker for the radio to come alive signaling enemy contact. Our Marines are deployed to numerous ambush sites anxiously awaiting the arrival of the enemy. They lie face down on the damp ground, frozen in silence and darkness with their weapons at the ready — not knowing what will happen next. Apprehension is relieved only in the belief in their capabilities as U.S. Marines and in the knowledge that their fellow Marines are nearby to cover their flanks and rear. They always know they are building on the Marine Corps tradition, and they aren't about to tarnish that image. Their waiting resembles a meditation period in prostrate yoga position. There is time now to reflect on a myriad of subjects, yet this luxury is marred by the necessity of having to maintain extreme alertness to the surroundings. Hours pass at an agonizing slow pace and discomfort intensifies. Any movement, even the slightest, might compromise their position and surprise. If any insect or animal crawls across your body, you leave it alone, hoping it eventually will leave. Snakes are of particular concern, but few are poisonous. If, however, a Vietnam pith viper bites you — you would be able to utter about one-half of an "Our Father" prior to dying. Rats are abundant, and, if one stops near your face, you simply stare it down. They generally are friendly and rarely bite. I'm certain you often wonder while lying there in the mud, "How in God's name did I end up in a rice paddy half way around the world?" Finally, if it begins to rain, the men have no recourse but to lie in the ever-increasing mud. Their entire bodies slowly become soaked, itchy and cool. It's a creepy feeling as the water seeks avenues to travel to every part of your body. Like tiny insects, the life-like water finds its way to places you wish were inviolate. There will be no relief from discomfort until first light.

At dawn when the opportunity allows them to move about, the very first thing the men do is to remove wet skivvies and socks. They have a dry pair inside a plastic sack in the field pack. Once on patrol again, they hang the wet socks on their cartridge belts allowing the sun to dry them. It is absolutely imperative that an infantryman keeps his feet dry. Constant wetness and moisture lead to emersion foot, which requires removal from the field. We do not have the luxury of losing personnel in this manner, as it will reduce our overall capability. We stress the point after conducting numerous supervisory inspections, thereby defusing the problem. We enjoy great small unit leadership from our junior officers and NCO's, who constantly look out for the men under their command. Their job is by no means very easy, and, in effect, they play nursemaid to many.

Without warning, the radio lights up with an excited and emotional voice reporting significant enemy contact. I grab the radio and answer the call — startled from the silence that has lulled me into semi-consciousness. The patrol leader reports that they have a large enemy unit under fire and have launched numerous flares for light. They actually can see the enemy soldiers dropping in their murderous fire. They have caught the Viet Cong by total surprise and virtually destroy the entire enemy unit. The firefight rages for several minutes, then falls off as the flares gradually extinguish. The return enemy fire ceases. I inform the patrol leader to stay put and that I will join them at dawn to assess the situation.

We leave Phu Bai prior to sunrise — you definitely need to see this. We don't have to travel far. The ambush site is outside one of the villages. After parking the jeep just off the road, we skirt the outside of the village to avoid people contact. We soon locate the battlefield and establish radio contact with our patrol. The eastern sky has turned orange as we approach the carnage. An eerie mist lingers just above the ground. Our canvas boots soak up the dew that had been chilling our feet. There is total silence — no immediate evidence of the pitched battle hours earlier. As I reach the patrol site, we make physical contact with our unit as they are arising to assess the situation. Several men move onto the killing field. I watch them as the sun begins burning away the mist, illuminating numerous bodies lying in contorted positions all over the area. They have dealt the VC a major setback!

I begin debriefing the patrol leader, not paying much attention to the Marines moving among the dead. What does catch my eye are two of our men reaching down pulling up the shirt on one of the bodies. Wondering what the hell is going on, I move in their direction. As I approach, I realize they are hovering over a dead women and have jerked up her shirt to expose her breasts! Two other men are doing the same thing nearby. I yell at all of them, asking what the hell they think they are doing! One Marine responds saying, "We want to see if her boobs are 34-36-38 / A-B-C or D."

I respond by saying, "For God's sake, men, we are in this country to assist them, not to debase their women. Let's not sink to the level of barbarians. Show some respect for the dead!"

There is no excuse for this kind of behavior, but you must bear in mind that these are young men shipped 8,000 miles from home to a dangerous foreign wilderness. None of them is even sure if he will ever make it back home. Just hours before, they were engaged in the heinous act of killing the enemy. Yet, in this environment, they are expected to revert quickly to the compassionate soldier. Furthermore, the people they are supposedly "protecting" are trying to kill them. The dead women were serving as supply carriers for the VC units. After this incident, we give a stern warning to all of our units not to repeat this sort of behavior in the future.

This is precisely an example of why I don't want American women on the front lines. War brings out both the best and the worst in men. In a highly dangerous, life-threatening situation, man often reverts to more primitive behavior, thereby revealing his darker animal nature. It's bad enough that men behave this way — do we really wish our society hardened further by putting weapons in women's hands and having them kill other mothers or sweethearts? No nation has incorporated such thinking into its military. Our society would be altered forever, and I don't believe we would like the ultimate results. Remember that these Vietnamese women are defending their country from what they believe are foreign invaders — similar to their experience with the French colonialists. After all, we are in the middle of a civil war. In addition, many Vietnamese women are pressed into service because the Viet Cong terrorize, assassinate and hold their family members hostage.

If we start bringing American woman home in body bags, the feminist drive to put women on the front lines will wither quickly. In their ultimate pursuit for absolute equality, women do not have the firsthand military combat experience to help in making a valid judgment about serving on the front lines. Many will reverse their decisions if they directly experience the carnage of war. Women should talk to any infantryman who participated in the World War II Battle of the Bulge in December 1944. The soldiers describe it as a "butcher shop" — blood filled their foxholes and pieces of their blown-up buddies fell on and clung to their own bodies. We sustained 70,000 casualties. Also, remember Gettysburg with 50,000 casualties. Our women will not be in deadly battle with other women, but with males from far less liberal cultures than ours. If captured on the battlefield, rape and torture will be their fate. No "social engineering," fairness or compassion exists in survival face-to-face combat. The Viet Cong brutalize the South Vietnamese women repeatedly.

Defending American soil is another story altogether. Women of all nations have come to the forefront to do *whatever* necessary to save their children, families and homes. I'm sure you would, too! But I'm talking about our foreign military policy, not a life-or-death defense of our families in our own homeland. Women should not have to experience the horrors of combat, unless no other alternative exists.

Chapter 7

DOC, WHY IS HE IN SO MUCH PAIN?

EACH PLATOON OR PATROL UNIT moves along daylight patrol routes in close proximity to a village and along avenues of approach to a village or built-up areas. The Patrol Leader selects an ambush site at a point somewhere along the patrol route. Just prior to darkness, they circle back to the same site and set up an ambush line and defensive perimeter. They set our claymore mines, which are directional explosives that send shrapnel in the direction they are pointed — truly devastating devices! Once again, it is hard to depict how bad the fury of war can get unless you have been there.

By 9 p.m. all the patrols report that they are in their ambush positions. About two hours later, our command bunker receives another excited radio communication. One of the 2nd Lieutenants has ventured out beyond the defensive perimeter and gets disoriented. He returns to the position from a different direction, but the Marines on the perimeter are not aware of this. Two — just two — shots ring out. The Lieutenant is hit.

The Patrol Leader asks for a med-evac helicopter. Our Air Officer submits the request, and, in a relatively short time, the chopper picks up the Lieutenant. While the chopper is enroute to the medical unit aboard the Phu Bai base, I head that way to see how he is doing. This is a good opportunity for you to come along and see an updated MASH unit in operation (remember the Korean War "MASH" series on TV).

When we walk into the facility, we are escorted directly to the

Lieutenant's bed. The doctor is standing alongside the Lieutenant as he screams with pain. He has been shot unbelievably in both kneecaps. I ask the doctor why he is in so much pain, but he ignores the question until he finishes examing the x-rays. As he holds them up to the lighted panel, I am totally shocked. Both kneecaps and all the bones in the knees are disintegrated into a thousand little pieces. I feel so sorry for the young man. It is that damn M-16 high velocity, low-weight bullet. It shatters everything upon entry.

The doctor informs me that both legs need to be removed at the knees. There is no way they can reconstruct his knees. It's one of the ugliest things I've ever seen. War touches and affects so many people and obviously has changed this young man's life forever! Everyone in our battalion could face a similar tragedy at any given moment. You only hope the percentages are in your favor and then you pray for those afflicted.

Chapter 8

WE NEED MORE BODIES!

THE TREMENDOUS SIZE of our Tactical Area of Responsibility is beginning to weigh on my mind. We are aggressive in our patrolling, covering a reasonable portion of the TAOR; however, we wish to cover more. This will require the organization of smaller-sized units and represents a calculated risk. We could jeopardize their ability to defend themselves adequately if they encounter a larger force.

Then the VC strikes, which creates another problem. They blow up two key bridges along Route 1 temporarily halting vehicular movement through the center of our TAOR. This doesn't pose a major threat to our units in the field because we can resupply and support them via helicopter. However, it does present a problem for commercial Vietnamese traffic. It also makes us look as though we have lost control and can't defend the loyal South Vietnamese villages. In the strategy of trying to win the hearts and minds of the Vietnamese people, we need to act fast and regain the initiative.

The engineers quickly erect makeshift portable bridges adjacent to the downed ones. These events exacerbate the problem, because now we need to protect the new bridges to keep the road open. Of course, that means more Marine personnel. Now we must try to increase patrol activity, cover more territory, and institute guard duty on the two bridges. The solution is up to me, as the boss asks me to draft a plan for immediate execution. This is a good time for you to consider what actions you

Blown bridge on Route 1 near Thon An Nong

might take. Do we forget being thorough and simply do the best we can? Do we ask Division HQ for another Marine infantry unit? Maybe we should even ignore a section of the TAOR so that we can do a better job in the remainder?

I'm not going to forget it because, like my hero General George Patton, I subscribe to "L'audace, l'audace, toujours l'audace" (audacity, audacity, always audacity)! Besides, I know full well that Division cannot spare another infantry unit anywhere. What we need is something unusual, creative and readily achievable. Then it dawns on me — task organization. This is a term with which you may or may not be familiar, but it is sufficient to say it consists of all the various combat support and combat service support units attached to a Marine infantry unit, depending on the mission. It can include tank, artillery, reconnaissance, sniper, engineer, medical, motor vehicle units, etc. In fact, our battalion already has some support units task organized to assist us; however, not many, because of our current mission.

I carefully go over the Operations Order for the 3rd Marine Division to ascertain all the unit types attached and actually in country. My plan is to tap those resources by requesting assignment of additional personnel from whoever would bite. We hurriedly draft a message to the Engineer Battalion informing them of our need for more engineers to assist with bridge repair and mine clearance. We draft another message to the Artillery Battery indicating we need more FO's (Forward Observers, who call in artillery support) for an expected increase in enemy contact due to the bridges being destroyed. And, we draft yet another message to the Sentry Dog Platoon advising them of the necessity to protect the bridges. To our utter amazement and delight, we receive return communiqués from all three organizations — the requested personnel are on the way. It appears that no other units have asked for such support and the men are in their billeting areas awaiting assignment. They soon will learn how comfortable they had been!

Within two days they begin arriving at the Phu Bai airfield: six sentry dogs with their handlers (I wanted the handlers), ten engineers, and four FO's. For us, that represents 20 new bodies, and that's just short of an infantry platoon. We are in business and will be able to do our job. Three dogs and their handlers are assigned to each of the temporary bridges for security. The dogs run free inside the barbed wire that protects land entry at each entrance and will alert the Marines of any breeches in the wire. Plus, they scare the hell out of Charlie. We also split the engineers, putting five at each bridge for security. We then assign one four-man fireteam from two infantry companies to create a very respectable Marine security unit of 12 people and three dogs. At the same time, it is a calculated risk that this size unit can actually protect the bridges. In defense of the bridges, we authorize the dropping of hand grenades off the sides, especially if the guards see bubbles. Charlie does use underwater demolition teams to destroy our bridges. This decision, however, leads to a very grievous event, as one of the Marines pulls a grenade pin and throws the grenade in a swinging hook-shot motion off the bridge. The grenade actually hits a support girder and bounces back at him. It must have startled him, because his immediate response is to cradle it next to his right leg. When it explodes, he loses most of his leg, but lives. What a lamentable accident. It is our second serious leg casualty. There will be others. This demonstrates the kind of capricious, random act that happens in war that changes human lives forever.

Notwithstanding this tragedy, the 20 additional personnel does allow us to move ahead with more patrols; albeit, with slightly smaller units than before. In addition, these actions allow us to cover a greater area. This should pay off handsomely in the future.

Chapter 9

WHERE'D THEY GO?

AS WE MOVE into November, the new patrol program is working like a charm. We have more patrols out, the VC/NVA have pulled back, the bridges appear secure, and no more enemy mortar fire has hit the Phu Bai Combat Base since we activated the aggressive patrolling and ambush effort. All the men continue to perform their duties admirably. Each night we have anywhere from 20 to 24 ambush sites established. "Charlie" damn well knows that we are prepared and await his movements. I honestly believe we are winning control.

Then all this activity seems to come to fruition. I note on the COC situation map that there are unusual concentrations of ambush sites in close proximity to one of the larger villages only about four miles south of Phu Bai Base. Around midnight, the radio, which has been stone silent, clicks on with a whispering voice. It is one of the ambush sites reporting very quietly that an extremely large VC unit is passing directly in front of them and moving towards the village. They are too formidable to engage. I plot their location and direction and confirm that they are in point of fact going towards the heart the village.

This is exciting because it presents us with a unique opportunity. Since we have a large number of sites adjacent to this village, I feel that if we move quickly to block all avenues of egress so that we virtually surround the village, we might score a major victory. One-by-one we contact the ambush leaders and assign them new positions outside the

Lt. Colonel Chaplin, Commanding Officer, and Captain John Martikke, S-4 Logistics Officer 2/26, at Phu Bai Base after battalion staff meeting

village — that is, if they are not already in position. We actually have enough Marines to do the job and the leaders are excellent in their execution. They all make it secretly to their newly assigned positions. There is no moon so it is pitch black. Nevertheless, after you are acclimated to the darkness, you really do get a feel for night operations. Unit leaders actually can identify every man in their unit when they are silhouetted against the horizon. Additionally, movement under the cover of darkness offers greater safety. We will use this tactic in future operations, as does Charlie.

The Battalion Commander is excited because he too feels that we have executed beautifully and are presented with a golden opportunity. I am definitely "pumped." This is the culmination of past tactical training and a reward for all of our hard work up to this point. We head out prior to daylight, and, since the travel distance is relatively short, arrive outside the village as an orange glow lights up the morning sky. There isn't a cloud in sight; conditions are perfect for a resounding military victory. We give the command to cordon off the village. Over 150 veteran U.S. Marines move simultaneously, creating a choke hold around the village. By now, Charlie has to know we are there — and in strength! Again, I wait anxiously for the first volley of fire, or, maybe even a white flag of surrender. Their position is totally untenable.

The three of us, the Colonel, you and I are standing by our command jeep with maps spread out over the hood. Funny how the mind works — it reminds me of a scene from the movie "March to Glory," which also depicted a Marine Battalion Commander poised over a map on the hood of a jeep. This is a similar situation; however, our temperature is around 65 degrees, while at the Chosin Reservoir in Korea it was below zero! This keeps things in perspective and makes the unbearable humidity and heat of Vietnam much more tolerable. Things can always be worse!

What happens next astonishes us. From several different directions of the village come scattered groups of men, maybe three to five per group, all just walking around heading nowhere. Furthermore, they are dressed in Sunday or holiday clothing — yet it is a weekday! Several small groups sit down and stretch out on the embankments along the village side of Route 1 until quite a crowd gathers. They talk among themselves, gesture at one another, and steal several glances in our direction. There is little doubt in my mind these are all VC. Some even have the audacity to walk over to the jeep and stand around watching us. They wear a very pleased expression on their faces — a few even smile. It also runs through my mind that, since many of them have congregated along the road, they are a perfect target. If circumstantial evidence is enough to convict in a U.S. courtroom, then perhaps this Vietnam courtroom would find them guilty of being our enemy. This then would be justification to inflict the death penalty on these obvious Viet Cong men. However, it is just a passing thought. It would be morally reprehensible. It does point out, nonetheless, the perverse thoughts that race through one's mind when totally frustrated and defeated. It is a Mexican standoff — the opportunity for victory evaporates and it proves to be a bizarre lesson. We search the village thoroughly and find absolutely nothing. The villagers either freely gave the Sunday clothing to the Viet Cong soldiers or they were coerced into providing the disguises. Either way, the weapons probably are at the bottom of the stream running through the village or concealed somewhere that we never uncover. Doesn't this punctuate the folly of war and the uniqueness of the Vietnam experience! We pack up and leave.

As we drive north, I begin to evaluate and analyze the many frustrating encounters, near misses, and lost opportunities because of restrictive

rules of engagement. Every day our unit demonstrates commitment, tenacity, patience and a great attitude. I sense now that the tactics of winning the confidence of the South Vietnamese and protecting their villages in our TAOR are flawed! If this is all we do throughout South
Vietnam, the war will drag on without a decisive outcome. After all, the
Viet Minh of the North started their war against the colonial French for
reunification in 1946 — 21 years earlier. I am all too familiar with his-
torical oriental patience, so I now hope for a major tactical change focused on defeating the North.

Chapter 10

COLONEL, I DON'T THINK I SHOULD LEAVE!

ONE DAY IN EARLY NOVEMBER I receive a message from the Red Cross informing me that my grandmother, Ruby Steenport, had died. I was very close to her, since she had actually acted as my surrogate mother — my "mom" since the age of three. Although the news is tragic, it isn't a total shock, as she had suffered minor heart problems for several years. I feared when I left for Vietnam that I might never see her again. She and my grandfather, Henry, reared me for ten years after my biological mother's divorce, when my mother moved to New York to pursue a modeling career. I moved into my grandparents' home and shared a room with their son, John (who is actually my uncle, although he is only four years older than I am). It was an exciting childhood growing up in a small Wisconsin town. Chilton had everything a young boy could want — river, woods, fishing, camping, firemen's picnics, freedom, and loving parents.

I had last seen Ruby at a family get-together at Lake Michigan in the summer of 1967 just prior to my Vietnam tour. Normally the military doesn't grant leave for a family death, unless it's an immediate parent or "loco parentis." I could invoke "loco parentis" since Ruby had raised me for ten years — the question is, "Can I really afford to go?" Of course, I want to go, but I have my duties to consider. I don't want to leave my fellow Marines in a lurch. I express my concern about leaving to Colonel Chaplin, and he emphatically responds, "You absolutely should go. You would always regret not going and we won't lose the Vietnam War while you're gone." His sage advice assuages my self-made guilt and I make arrangements to depart. Marines do watch out for one another. You, however, will remain in Vietnam awaiting my return in one week. Try to stay out of trouble.

After catching a chopper to DaNang, I board a C-5 military transport to California. Shortly after landing at Travis AFB, I catch a commercial flight to Milwaukee, where my aunt picks me up for the drive to Chilton, Wisconsin for the funeral. I recently have been promoted to Major, but the excitement obviously is subdued due to this tragic loss. I wear my Marine Corps uniform to the funeral, as this is all the clothing I have for the trip, and Ruby was proud of my being commissioned in the Marines. This is one of the saddest days in my life and a terrible loss. I always will recall her memory with love. Standing at her graveside, I know that I had made the right decision to be at her funeral. I both needed and wanted to return the love and respect she so deserved and gave me so freely.

After the services, I return to St. Louis with my parents for a quick visit. It is disappointing that neither time nor money allow my wife and son to make a hurried return to the states to be with me at this time. When the emergency leave runs out, I catch a military transport flight back to Vietnam. The juxtaposition of being shot at in Vietnam one day and then standing in a church in the Midwest the next seems absolutely unreal. It was a good sort of "culture shock." My tour of duty has just begun, but I already am missing my family and the states. I can't say that I'm eager to return to green Vietnam, but we've got a job to do.

Chapter 11

FEAR, CHAOS, VALUES AND SOUL SEARCHING

I THOUGHT LONG AND HARD about relating this incident to you, as my fellow Marines might misconstrue the event as denigrating to our cherished Corps officer corps. However, the more I reflected on the circumstances, the more I felt it portrays the deepest emotional makeup of any human being and his response to fear, chaos, death, values and responsibility. It's a human story that needs telling.

Upon returning from emergency leave in November 1967, I visit Command Headquarters in Okinawa the day before my flight back to Vietnam. Walking down the hall, I encounter another Marine Major and former classmate of mine at the Amphibious Warfare School in Quantico, Virginia in the spring of 1967. We actually sat next to one another in the classroom on several occasions. He is a poster-looking Marine officer with an enviable record of key assignments. He even sports jump wings and served in one of our renowned reconnaissance units. He certainly has all the credentials.

When I recognize him I stop to engage him in conversation. I am puzzled by the expression on his face, as he seems stunned and bewildered. I ask him how and what he is doing. He shocks me by saying he is on his way home as he just had resigned from the Corps! I don't feel I should press him for details and extend him my best wishes before we part ways.

I later learn what happened, and, once I know some details, it makes me reflect long and hard. I realize I can't be too judgmental of his conduct because I've always felt that each individual is unique with different strengths, weaknesses and values. Like me, he had been assigned as Operations Officer for a Marine Infantry Battalion operating somewhere south of Con Thien. As the unit moved over the terrain, they were taken under heavy enemy mortar fire and sustained numerous casualties. When the fatalities mounted, this Marine Major became confused, concerned and disoriented. He informed the Battalion Commander of the gravity of the situation, but seemed frozen, unable to do anything. The CO instructed him to "get it together" and told him that he would join him shortly. When the CO arrived, the Major informed him that he simply couldn't take all the death and chaos; whereupon, the CO relieved him of his duties on the spot and sent him to the rear. He later was called before the Commanding General of the 3rd Marine Division, who read him the "riot act" and dressed him down severely. The General gave him a choice of a court martial or resignation. The Major chose the latter.

My encounter with him is during his final leg on the way out of the Marine Corps. I subsequently hear several derogatory comments about the Major, but I discount them. No one knows what his reaction will be when faced with combat. Fear grips everyone — all you can do is to grapple with it to regain control. If you are unable to do so, there simply isn't much you or anyone can do about it. War is brutal. Some people just can't contend with the savage reality and choose not to partake in it — no matter what the consequences. Those who adjust, overcome and survive will have conquered fear for the remainder of their lives.

I frankly will not judge anyone who cannot deal with the fear, calamity and chaos of man's stupidest adventure. It's better they learn this as soon as possible and leave the military before they put others at risk. There are many more civilized ways of serving your country. I sincerely hope he can put this negative and unfortunate experience behind him and press on with a productive life that suits him — instead of feeling a failure as a man. Some people might say, "Survival of the fittest," but "fittest for what"! I never hear more.

Chapter 12

OH HELL! WE'RE DEAD!

WE ARE ENTERING the final week of November, when I receive a directive from Division Headquarters. They order us to move one of our four rifle companies over to protect a Vietnamese rock quarry. This site is at least 15 miles west of Hue City — actually outside our current TAOR. Unfortunately, this means a major shift in our troop deployment and overall tactical screen. Activities in the northern sector of our TAOR,

The imperial cannons near the former old national capital of Vietnam in Hue.

Market in Hue City

which stop at Hue, would increase.

I accompany the Company out to the quarry site and watch the Company Commander set up his defensive perimeter. I note that there is a Special Forces camp further west along the Perfume River. I decide to visit them to see if I can get a feel for the territory. They are very receptive and we have a cordial visit, but I don't learn anything of value before returning to Phu Bai.

Since we are going to be more active in the north, I also decide to visit Hue City. The new assistant S-3 Officer, Captain Piper, and I set out north. As usual, we take our two jeeps and drivers. Hue, the ancient capital of Vietnam, is very picturesque with wide-treed avenues and a historic imperial fortress. Upon arrival, we stop at the Hue Chief of Police Headquarters and talk to the Chief and two American Police Advisors to the Vietnamese city government. They are from the Los Angeles Police Department and volunteered to help advise and train the Hue City police force for one year. They go into great detail telling about their bachelor pad on the outskirts of Hue where they live with very attractive Vietnamese women. The Vietnamese are a handsome people. There also has been a lot of intermarriage and liaisons between the local Vietnamese and French Army occupiers prior to our involvement. The children of these unions are oftentimes stunning. I wonder how the Vietnamese will treat the American-Vietnamese children when we leave. These guys feel they are living the good life far from danger. In Vietnam, the picture can turn ugly in short order. The visit proves interesting, but, again, we learn very little.

As we drive around, we stop at the old historic temple site in the middle of Hue. This visit almost causes a major tragedy and embarrassment! Each of our jeeps has long whip antennas attached to the left rear of the jeep to ensure good radio communications. As we travel the streets of Hue, we occasionally encounter low hanging wires and reach out routinely to pull down the antennas so they won't hit. As we approach one of the major intersections in the city, we again depress the antennas. Captain Piper is in front of me and does not notice the policeman standing on a traffic box in the middle of the intersection. The jeep passes immediately next to the stand, and, as he pulls the antenna down and forward, his arm is extended just outside the left side of the jeep. As he rushes by, the steel antenna comes within a mere six inches of spearing the policeman at heart level. It would have pierced the police officer like a lance in a

Captain Piper directs our drivers to break down our whip antennas after our near disaster in Hue.

medieval jousting match! Since we have seen most of the city and we don't want to do any more damage, we call it a day. Besides, it is getting late and we want to head down Route 1 to Phu Bai prior to darkness.

My next trek is back to the rock quarry to stay in touch with our outlying unit. Cohesiveness is important in any war. This time I take only my driver and you. Just after getting underway I strap myself securely into the jeep so I won't fall out while sleeping. Since I am awake most nights until 1:00 or 2:00 a.m. and up at 5:00 or 6:00 a.m., I don't get much sleep. Therefore, the habit of taking naps during all my jeep trips becomes a necessity. Many Marines wonder how I can relax enough to sleep on the Vietnam roads — the answer is exhaustion. Catching shut eye whenever possible is high upon on the hierarchy of survival. I am fast asleep, when the next thing we hear is, "Oh hell, we're dead!" Now that will wake you up in a hurry! We are ten miles southwest of Hue City in "no man's land."

As I regain consciousness, what I see almost stops my heart! Coming out of a forested area about 50 yards up the road is a whole military

River boats on the Perfume River in Hue on October 20, 1967, two months prior to the TET offensive.

unit dressed in black pajamas. Do you happen to know what uniform "Charlie" sports? We cannot stop, nor would we want to do so. Consequently, we plow right into the middle of the group. They casually step aside. I don't have guts enough to look back, figuring that we are indeed dead! Unlike General George Patton, I don't want to see the bullet coming. To our grateful surprise and relief, no shots ring out; we are in luck. They must have been South Vietnamese troops. We later learn they were a special unit of the ARVN (Army of the Republic of Vietnam) named the Black Panthers operating in the vicinity. Running around the contested "no man's land" definitely is fraught with dangers. We're pushing our luck.

Chapter 13

A SECOND BRUSH WITH DEATH

THIS TIME I happen to be spending the day in the field somewhere in our TAOR just observing patrol operations and showing the command flag. We have been walking quite a distance and decide to stop to rest. The Company Commander and his command group are about a hundred yards ahead of my small group, so you and I head over to his area alone.

It has been sunny, but a scattered thundershower moves into the area just prior to our break. As we walk those hundred yards, it not only is lightning and pouring down sheets of rain, but ground water is starting to build up. I don't know about you, but I hate lightning. It always frightened me as a youngster, and I know hunters and golfers who were struck while in the field. We now are standing ankle deep in a small pond when suddenly lightning strikes nearby. The only thing I recall is being on my knees, my heart pounding madly and the end of my fingers tingling. Lightning has hit the ground nearby, running through the water and has knocked us down. You are on your knees, too, and you don't have to say a word. We feel fortunate to be alive. So far we've had to deal with "Charlie," the NVA, and now "Mother Nature." Just be happy that we're still alive, because we've just had a second brush with death!

Chapter 14

MAC ARTHUR REVISITED

WE NOW HAVE a new Battalion Commander, Lt.Colonel Frank Heath. We even schedule a change of command parade in his honor on a rainy day in early December and bring back the closest Rifle Company to Phu Bai for the ceremony. Coupled with another of our companies currently

Change of command parade at Phu Bai for Lt. Colonel Frank Heath, the new Battalion Commander, and Lt. Colonel Duncan Chaplin

in Phu Bai, we have a nice turnout for Lt. Colonel Heath's and Lt. Colonel Duncan Chaplin's change of command ceremony. Immediately following his assumption of command, I thoroughly brief Lt. Colonel Heath on past and current operations. He quickly grasps the situation and endorses our patrolling operations.

It is about noon three weeks later — until now the day is warm and uneventful. As I'm working at my desk in the COC, one of our Second Lieutenant Platoon Leaders walks into the bunker directly to my desk. I look up, greet him and ask what he wants. "Major, I want your advice," is his opening comment. I always enjoy assisting our junior officers and respond, "Pull up a chair, Lieutenant. How can I help?"

He begins his story, "Sir, I just received a set of orders posting me to Camp Pendleton, California, which I personally do not mind. However, I was just married prior to my tour in Vietnam, and my wife is from North Carolina. She is not happy being ordered to California; but rather hoped I would get orders to Camp Lejeune after Vietnam. I am thinking of making the Corps my career, but my wife wants to be nearer her family for now. Is there anything I can do?"

My immediate thought is that I definitely want to keep this promising young officer in the Marine Corps. He performs his duties well and offers great promise. I reply, "Lieutenant, this should not be an insurmountable obstacle. I'll draft a letter to your detailer at HQ Marine Corps for the CO's signature requesting a switch with another officer. I'm certain that there is an officer who has been ordered to Lejeune who would prefer sunny California. If we pull this off, will you stay in the Corps for three more years and consider a career?" He snaps back crisply, "Yes, Sir," and thanks me for my concern as he departs.

I prepare a rough draft for typing that I place in the corner of my desk. It just got dark outside and I spot the CO entering the COC. He requests to see the ambush sites we had established for the night on the situation map, which is located next to my desk. One of the Patrol Leaders checks in on the communication net, and I turn to acknowledge the information.

When I look back, the CO is reading my letter for the Lieutenant's change of orders and indicates his refusal to sign it. I was shocked at his response because I hold respect for this man and wish to agree with his thinking. I try to explain that the Lieutenant is an asset the Corps should retain, but he felt obliged to consider his young wife's wish to remain near her home for the time. The CO listens, pauses and then replies that the young man needs to execute his orders — that his duty is to serve the Corps. I respectfully disagree. With a look of disappointment, he asks me about my own priorities. I answer, "My order of precedence is God, family, country and the Corps. His reply hurts, "Then maybe you should consider not making the Corps a career." Time to clam up — this has gone further than I intended or expected. It is a closed issue. We all do not think alike. Every man makes his choices in life and embraces his own hierarchy of values. Mine happen to be the same as General Douglas MacArthur's priorities and I hold them with no apologies.

I enjoy serving in the Marine Corps with so many true professionals. However, there is a large part of the officer corps that feels that the number one priority in their lives is the Corps. Personally, I feel that a man will fight harder to protect his family, before country or military loyalty. Perhaps one exception would be the French Foreign Legion, which is comprised of many men who hold allegiance to nothing else. This just demonstrates the strong need to belong to something to give meaning to life.

Let me tell you about another incident as an example of this primary focus on the Corps. During the 1966 Christmas holidays in Quantico, Virginia, a group of Captains, who were instructors at the Basic School for newly commissioned officers, asked if I wanted to join them on a trip to Fort Benning, Georgia, to attend a crash parachute jump course to earn jump wings. In so doing, we would be away from our families for most of the Christmas holidays. When I opted out, saying I wanted to spend time with my family, you would have thought I committed heresy! My thinking was that there would be many forced separations from family in the future and why elect for an additional one.

The Lieutenant did end up leaving the Corps. We lost a good man.

Chapter 15

THERE'S NO DOUBT IN MY MIND THEY'RE COMING

WE JUST CELEBRATED a quiet and lonely Christmas party in the COC Bunker. With only cake and soft drinks, you certainly can't confuse it with a home-style Christmas. The next year — 1968 — is ushered in with even less fanfare. I realize I will be 32 years old in August and that Alexander the Great and Jesus died at 33. I certainly don't pretend to be in their league, but it strikes me how young they were when they passed from history.

Our deployment in early January sees us spread out even more, but with an increased emphasis on the area between Phu Bai, Hue and the rock quarry. Our company at the quarry is abreast one of the major avenues of approach to Hue from the west. The western edge of our TAOR is hilly and fairly heavily treed, but opens up for approximately ten miles until Hue City. We begin heavy patrolling in this area of trees, shrubs and cemeteries.

In short order, we again encounter the enemy. One of our patrols runs headlong into theirs at night. Can you imagine the response of those two point patrol members when confronting each other? Fortunately, our guy fires first and survives. The encounters occur more frequently and I begin to see a pattern. Their patrols always head toward Hue City and something has to be happening. I inform Colonel Heath, "I think that they are coming — with Hue the probable target." The contacts are so numerous now that all doubt in my mind has evaporated. They are planning to hit Hue! We are so convinced, that we initiate a request to 3rd Marine Division Headquarters for an Archlight (B-52 bombing strike) on the wooded area where we believe they are massing. Ironically, by Division's response, you would have thought that we asked for 30-days R&R (Rest and Recuperation) in Australia. They summarily deny the request.

Next a major event occurs. We receive notification from Division Headquarters that the entire 5th Marine Regiment is taking over our TAOR and we are ordered to join our parent unit, the 26th Marine Regiment at Khe Sanh. We are to "enplane" in a week.

The 5th Marine Regiment is legendary in the Marine Corps. It won accolades at Belleau Wood in World War I, Guadacanal in World War II, and the Chosin Reservoir in Korea. I already had been the Executive Officer of Fox Company, 2nd Battalion, 5th Marines in 1961-62 when I captained their rifle and pistol team in the Western Division rifle matches in 1961. They are a proud outfit; you can be sure of that. However, this time they are a little too proud.

The Battalion Commander and I schedule a meeting with the 5th Marine Regimental staff, with my focus on their S-3 Operations officer. A regiment consists of three infantry battalions and the Headquarters Company. We are a level down and that seems to become an important issue. I do the briefing to their Commanding Officer and S-3. I lay out our deployment effort since last August and home in on the results. I end with a current analysis of the encounters and engagements in the northern sector of the TAOR and serious nature of the threat on Hue. They look at each other with amazement when I mention our request for an Archlight on the nearby hills.

They are polite, but unimpressed as they say, "The 5th Marines are here now." As you sit there with me, do you perceive some arrogance and a failure to listen — even a downright dismissal? Well, I do, so I end my conversation with the S-3 with a prediction. I tell him that if they don't give credence to our briefing and emulate our patrol strategy in the TAOR, mortars (or worse) will fall on Phu Bai and Hue will be attacked within a week. Since my warnings are totally dismissed, I decide it is time to leave. We depart in two days for our destiny at Khe Sanh.

I'm proud of our unit's four-month performance; the Marine infantrymen were outstanding. This probably is the last time U.S. forces had control of the TAOR. Mortars land on Phu Bai within eight days, killing some pilots and other personnel. Hue falls in two more weeks. They are coming — it is the eve of the 1968 Tet Offensive! I wonder what would have happened if we had been proactive, rather than reactive. History does repeat itself when solid, accurate and timely intelligence information from the lower field units is ignored. General McArthur learned this the hard way in 1950 when Marine infantry units told him the Chinese had entered the war. He went into denial.

On January 30, the massive 1968 TET Offensive is launched in built-up areas throughout Vietnam. The two U.S. police advisors from Los Angeles are killed when their villa is overrun and Hue is captured. This brings on a bloody house-to-house battle. I lose several fellow Marine officers in the fight with whom I had served in the past. The NVA/VC even capture the woman who had been my barber in Phu Bai and hang her upside-down from a tree, cutting her throat and severing both her hands. The hands apparently are cut off because she had been a barber cutting their enemies' hair. There are so many needless casualties and sacrifices in this undeclared war!

Part II

KHE SANH

KHE SANH

WE LAND at Khe Sanh Combat Base mid-morning on January 16, 1968. Upon disembarking the C-130 transport aircraft, we assemble the battalion and proceed to a bivouac area about 1,000 meters west of the airfield. With our arrival, the 26th Marine Regiment is together as a combat unit for the first time since Iwo Jima in 1945. Lt. Colonel Heath, you and I head to the 26th Marine command bunker for a thorough briefing from regimental staff and for our assignment. On their large situation map, I note that we are 10 clicks (10,000 meters) from the Laotian border to the southwest and 26 clicks (26,000 meters) from the DMZ to the north. Khe Sanh is tucked in the very northwest corner of South Vietnam I Corps Tactical Area.

During the regimental briefing, we are told that all evidence indicates that the NVA is planning a major offensive in the Khe Sanh area. Apparently there are two NVA infantry divisions relatively close to our position. One of the divisions, the 304th, is considered an elite unit, having participated in the French defeat at Dien Bien Phu! In early January, a major intelligence coup occurs when six men dressed like U.S. Marines appear outside a Marine sentry post. When they fail to respond to repeated challenges from our troops, the Marines gun them down. Upon retrieving their bodies, we learn they are actually NVA officers — two of them being a Regimental Commander and his Operations Officer. Reconnaissance by key officers leads headquarters to conclude the NVA has targeted Khe Sanh for a major offensive. This event, plus other pieces of intelligence, led Marine General Cushman to transfer our

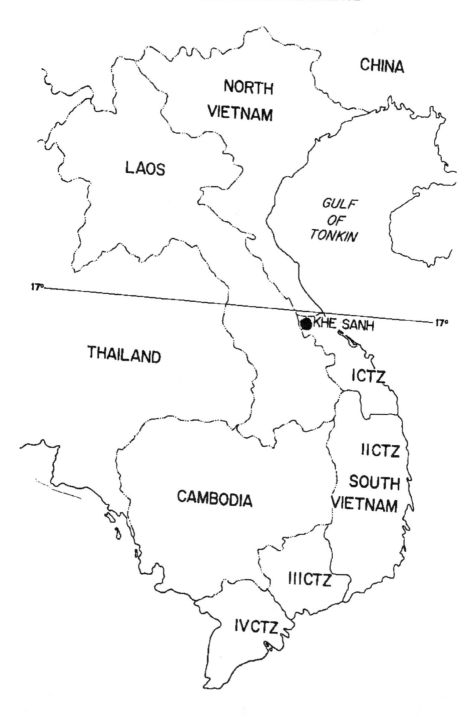

Indochina

unit to Khe Sanh on January 16.

Upon completion of the briefing, they order us to occupy and defend the Hill 558 complex — 3000 meters northwest of the Khe Sanh combat base. This move should block effectively the major avenue of approach to the base via the Rao Quan valley from the northwest. A major trail passes by Hill 558 on the way to the old French Plantation adjacent to the current Khe Sanh combat base. The trail actually turns into a road as it reaches the base on its way ultimately to Route 9.

It is now mid-afternoon and we know we cannot pick up the entire battalion, move north, and organize any viable defense prior to nightfall. However, we do want to take control of Hill 558 as soon as possible, so we notify Captain Chuck Divelbiss, Commanding Officer, F Company, to move his unit out immediately to occupy Hill 558. The rest of the

Khe Sanh Area

battalion prepares to bed down in the bivouac area about 500 meters west of the Khe Sanh Combat Base.

I begin to worry about F Company's situation, but this is dispelled as I receive Captain Divelbiss's radio transmission, "All went well, we are in position on the hill and battened down." Nothing more to do for the moment. Let's hit the sack.

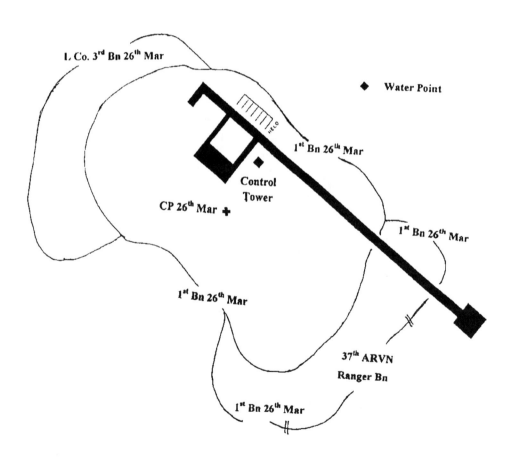

Khe Sanh Combat Base

Chapter 16

OUR FIRST FIREFIGHT, OR WAS IT?

AS DAYLIGHT DAWNS, we begin packing up the battalion for the move to join F Company on Hill 558. We finally get underway around 8 a.m., and, as we march overland, we encounter tall elephant grass, bushes and several trees. It's very still, humid and hot. I can't help thinking about how the area around the combat base had been a beautiful working plantation, but now the French are a mere afterthought. However, I am certain that we will fare better than our old ally. It does not take us long to traverse the 3,000 meters and join up with F Company. Once in position, we immediately set about establishing our defensive perimeter.

The perimeter we determine incorporates all of Hill 558 and the small hill just to the rear of 558 (see map). As we prepare our defenses, I study the map to get a feel for the adjacent terrain. There are key mountain peaks throughout the entire area. Hill 1015 is 3,000 meters east; Hill 950 is 2,000 meters to the northeast; Hill 861 is 2,000 meters almost due west; and Hill 881 south 4,000 meters to the west/southwest. Khe Sanh Combat Base is 3,000 meters to our southeast.

Lush foliage and some fairly tall trees cover the surrounding hill-sides. The Rao Quan River sparkles in the valley below steep riverbanks, some of them quite high. In fact, the western bank is part of our defensive perimeter to the east. A bowl is formed between the rear of Hill 558 and the small hill behind it. Our COC is established on the backside of Hill 558. The open area beyond the smaller hill to the south is primarily flat land, where fields of grass stand quite high in some regions. Overall, it is very calm and picturesque. (I include copies of my original Khe San operational map to show the terrain and unit deployments.)

As the sun sets on the first day on our new home around Hill 558, we still have plenty of work to do. The permanent defensive perimeter is delineated and the troops have dug their foxholes. Of course, they will continue to improve them in the days ahead. But, for now, we are at least underground.

It now is totally dark and all is quiet. At around 11 p.m. the quiet is interrupted by an initial volley of fire from our lines facing the Rao Quan River northeast of our positions. Within moments it is obvious that we are in a major firefight. Flares begin floating down on parachutes, which gradually lighten the midnight sky. The CO, you and I race from our command area to the perimeter position engaged in all the fire. We are laying down one hell of a volume of fire. But, what is strange about all this activity is that there doesn't seem to be any incoming or return fire from the enemy. As additional flares provide even more light, we begin to see more clearly. There is a lot of frantic movement on the eastern rock ledges across the Rao Quan River. However, to our amazement, they don't seem to be humans; rather, they are "rock apes" scrambling over the rocks! Much to our chagrin, we manage to have our first major firefight at Khe Sanh, albeit one way, with a bunch of monkeys. Thankfully, we don't suffer any casualties — only extreme embarrassment. We are very cryptic in our situation report to Regimental HQ, as they had heard and seen our activities from the Khe Sanh combat base. No one mentions this bizarre incident until time eases our chagrin and it begins to take a humorous slant. Just think — you are here to witness it — just don't tell anyone about it. This is only the beginning. Old man bizarre is alive and well.

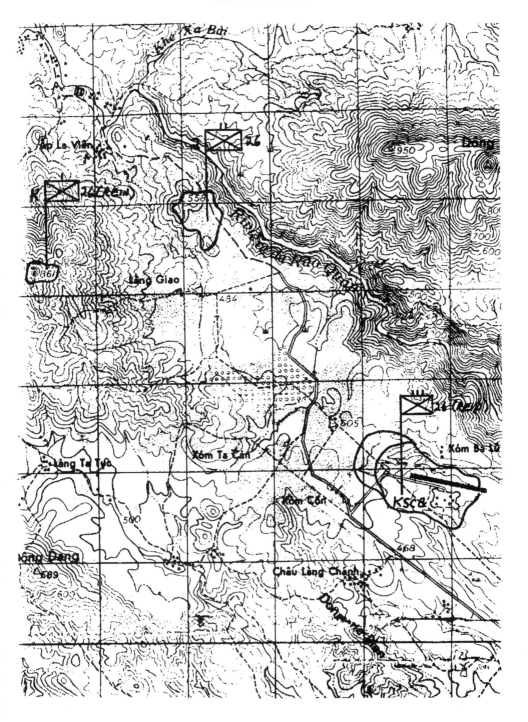

Hill 558, our new home

Chapter 17

L'AUDACE, L'AUDACE
WHAT DO YOU MEAN A SIEGE?

ON OUR SECOND DAY, we decide to look for the enemy. Towards this end, we establish a probing patrol plan. We break the patrol plan into sectors out in front of our position. If the NVA is there, it has to be somewhere in a 180-degree area directly to our front — that is, directly to our north. Remember that Hill 950 is across the river to the east and a company from 3rd Battalion 26th Marines is due west about 2,000 meters atop Hill 861. Therefore, the NVA has to be located to the area to the north. Our patrolling plan consists of three sectors. Starting in sector one, we will patrol each day of January 18, 19 and 20 (see map).

On January 18 we launch a reinforced platoon into Sector 1. I decide to accompany the patrol in order to get the lay of the land. An Infantry Operations Officer always needs to get a firsthand view of the terrain on which the battalion is fighting — a simple map inspection doesn't cut it. Anyway, you might enjoy a walk in the woods also. We move out early in the morning, cross the rocky Rao Quan riverbed and then climb the riverbanks to a flat area of deep, sharp grass in front of Hill 950. The men have to keep their utility sleeves rolled down to avoid some nasty cuts. This is additionally uncomfortable, since there is no wind and it is both sunny and hot. Despite these conditions, we traverse a fairly good-sized section of terrain by afternoon. However, we haven't encountered anything — no signs of NVA activity anywhere. Prior to sunset we set

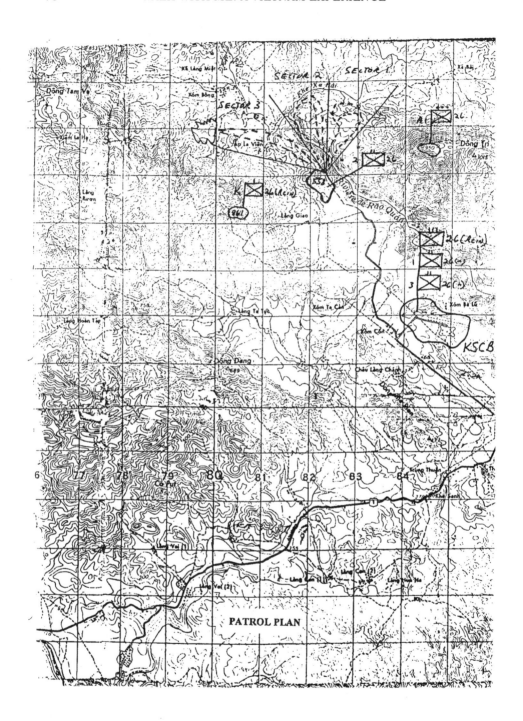

Patrol Plan

up a defensive position, cutting out fields of fire through the tall grass, and finally settle in for the night. The night seems to drag on forever. We are stuck out in front of everyone at Khe Sanh alone. I'm not even sure if we filed a patrol plan with Regimental HQ. At sunrise we pack up and head back taking a different route just to be on the safe side (patrols always do this to avoid anyone lying in ambush awaiting their return). We finally arrive back at Hill 558 — results, no NVA in Sector 1. You have to admit, however, that it proves to be a scenic stroll through the countryside.

The same day, January 19, we launch another patrol to check out Sector 2. This time, I feel the odds are increasing that we could encounter the enemy. I decide to stay back, as we are developing our defensive perimeter around Hill 558 — which is both essential and tedious. Much still needs to be done in order to ensure a formidable defensive position. The patrol plans to stay out only for the day, returning just before nightfall — that is, unless they run into the NVA. On schedule just prior to darkness, the patrol returns with the same results as the day before — no contact and no signs of the enemy. We are two-thirds done and I now am convinced thoroughly that they have to be located in Sector 3. This would put them in front of Hill 861. A survey of the map indicates these are some small hills about 3,000 meters out so we will move in that direction next, but with more force and even more caution.

On January 20, F Company leaves our perimeter around 4 a.m. and heads into Sector 3, where those small hills are located. Again, we mask our movement under the cover of darkness. But, I am totally unaware that I Company, 3rd Battalion, 26th Marines (commanded by my old classmate Captain Bill Dabney, who married the daughter of a Marine Corps legend Chesty Puller) also has moved out of their position on Hill 881S at 5 a.m. that morning, about an hour after F Company. They are headed toward Hill 881N about 1,000 meters north of its sister Hill 881S. They will end up engaged in a major battle with the NVA, which will last most of the day. Their engagement begins around 9 a.m. We are to engage an hour prior to that. Lt. Colonel Alderman and Major Caulfield (CO and S-3) are heli-lifted to Hill 881S around 9 a.m. on January 20 to assume operational control of their engaged units.

After approximately three hours, our patrol, moving with incredible

Drawing by Chris Kurth

stealth, starts to creep up the small slope in front of Hill 516 directly in front of Hill 861. Bingo — they spot the NVA soldiers' campsite. The enemy is rising for the morning, with some drinking coffee. Our units watch as a few of them shave in front of small mirrors hung in the trees. The area is fairly heavily wooded with lots of small shrubs and trees.

All hell breaks loose when we heave a bunch of hand grenades in their direction. We catch them totally by surprise, and, in the process, start the first offensive combat action of the Khe Sanh campaign! The NVA doesn't hesitate to regroup and return fire. We observe the whole operation through binoculars from Hill 558. You actually can see both sides firing, throwing grenades, and maneuvering their men. I am totally caught up in the action as I communicate with the Company Commander — he is doing an outstanding job. I tell him we can see the engagement as we have actual line-of-sight to the action. It is my first out-and-out, face-to-face daylight combat as a Marine officer, and we are totally prepared. I won't, however, be surprised if you are dumbfounded about now! It is moving fast and furious and it will get even faster.

In the radio communication, I tell the Company Commander that I have line-of-sight to one of the NVA positions that has engaged them. I believe that we can neutralize them by using one of our 106mm recoil-

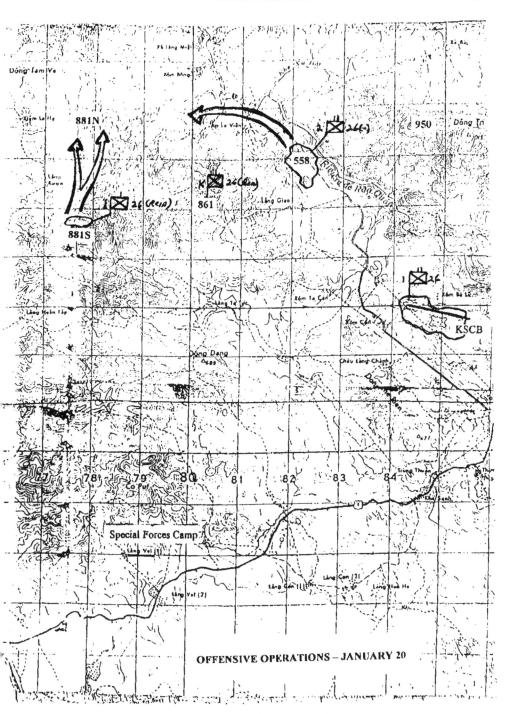

Offensive Operations — January 20

less rifles — a nasty and very accurate weapon. I run over to the weapons crew and point out the target to the gunners. They are confident that they can hit the mark. When they fire, the round heads directly for the enemy position. You can see and hear it spinning and whistling through the air. On impact, one NVA soldier is lifted several feet off the ground and thrown into the trees. I realize that it is the first human being whom I had a direct hand in killing and there are probably others. Now, you've also had your baptism by fire. The thought, "Thank heaven it wasn't me," races through my mind. This sure serves to personalize the war for me.

We have the NVA on the defensive and I am getting ready to reinforce F Company with yet another company — and also to call in some close air support. I receive a radio communication from Major Matt Caulfield, the S-3 of 3rd Battalion, 26th Marines, who is atop Hill 881S conducting their action. He suggests we coordinate our effort and attack them from the east. I totally concur; after all, military thought says, "L'audace, l'audace, toujours l'audace," and I am marshaling forces (a second rifle company) for yet another defeat of NVA forces. I conclude that if we run into an even larger force, we can still tear them up with our artillery and close air support (see map). Additionally, it might force Regiment to commit elements of 1st Battalion, 26th Marines — we are here to defeat the North, not dig trenches. Besides, as General Patton always said, "Fortified positions are monuments to the stupidity of man."

Then comes the most disheartening message that I ever receive in Vietnam! The Regimental Operations Officer orders us both to break contact, call in choppers, to evacuate our dead and wounded, and actually retreat back to hills 558 & 881S. In a combat situation, you don't ask questions, you don't beg for further consideration, you don't turn off your radio, you just obey the orders — even if you cannot comprehend them.

Once again F Company functions sharply and professionally as they disengage. The evacuation goes smoothly and in a timely fashion. We don't lose a single helicopter in the process. Once all our forces are back inside the wire, I contact Regiment to update them of our return. I can't help asking what was up? Their response still resonates in my mind to this day. The "higher-ups" had claimed that we were under siege. In reality, we were actually kicking the tar out of the NAV! We were taking

Khe Sanh Combat Base — Aerial photo taken January 28, 1968 by 460 Tactical Reconnaissance Wing, USAF

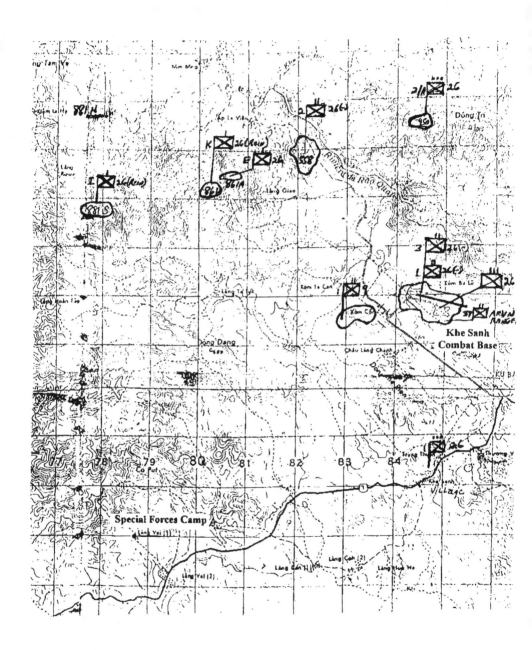

Deployment of 26th Marine Regiment (REIN) on January 30, 1978 (as plotted on original field map)

the war to them and we had the firepower to win — how and the hell did they think it was a siege?

I later learn that they had captured a NVA officer on January 20. He told Regiment that the NVA was preparing to attack on Hill 881S and 861 the very next day. He didn't mention Hill 588, but I doubt that they would attack us because we are far too strong. I have an entire Marine battalion at my disposal and we simply would have kicked their butts. In truth, you will see later just how prepared we were. I always will maintain that if I Company, 3rd Battalion, 26th Marines and F Company, 2nd Battalion, 26th Marines had not attacked on the 20th of January, we would have suffered far greater consequences. As it turns out, we probably disrupted their plans for a full-scale attack against numerous positions.

However, the NVA does launch an early morning attack on January 21st against K Co. 3rd Battalion, 26th Marines, atop Hill 861. Moving up the southwest side of Hill 861, they blow holes in the protective wire with bangaloor topcdos and swarm into K Company's position. Captain Norm Jasper (an instructor with me at the Basic School) is wounded several times and turns over command to his Executive Officer who coordinates a counterattack. Using any means at hand, rifles, knives, fists, grenades, the Marines drive the NVA from the hill, preserving their position. The whole encounter takes place 1700 meters west of our position on Hill 558 and 3000 meters northeast of I Company on Hill 881S. Had the NVA succeeded, it would have split out two hill positions and forced us to counterattack to regain our hill position integrity.

Command U.S. Forces Military Assistance Command Vietnam (COMUSMACV) Headquarters now is certain that a major confrontation is setting up around the hills of Khe Sanh. Therefore, reinforcements arrive on January 22 when Lt. Colonel Mitchell's 1st Battalion, 9th Marines arrive and are placed southwest of the base. On January 27, the 37th ARVN Ranger Battalion also arrives and is deployed along the eastern section of the defense perimeter at Khe Sanh base. I still feel we should have taken the initiative just prior to their TET offensive on January 30. When 1/9 arrives on January 22, we should have marshaled the forces of 1/9, 2/26 and 1/26 to form a potent strike force. Add a Marine tank company, employ devastating air support, and go out to get them on January 28. The 37th ARVN Ranger Battalion along with base support

General Leonard F. Chapman,
a USMC Commandant
U.S. Marine Corps

personnel (i.e., HQ Company, 26th Marines) and elements of 3/26 could have defended the base.

Had the NVA marshaled its forces for an attack on the combat base, our strike force could have defeated them. The Marines at the Chosin Reservoir in 1950 attacked against far greater odds. Had we seized the initiative, we well might have altered the TET offensive in the I Corps area. As General Carl VonClausewitz said, "For great aims we must dare great things."

On January 22, Captain Earl Breeding, CO of E Company, is moved to the high ground immediately to our west. This is intended to close the gap between Hill 558 and Hill 861. The new position is dubbed Hill 861A. Because it actually is closer to K Company, 3rd Battalion, 26th Marines on Hill 861, we pass operational control of our company to the 3rd Battalion a day later. In just a few short days, E Company also will receive its baptism by fire.

Sitting alone on the crest of Hill 950 surveying the entire Khe Sanh area and defending the radio relay site for crucial communications is the 2nd Platoon, A Company, 1st Battalion, 26th Marines. I learn that the Marine Corps Commandant's son, 1st Lieutenant Walt Chapman, is with the platoon. Lieutenant Chapman was a student in my Basic School Company in 1966/67 at Quantico, Virginia. His father, General Leonard Chapman, Commandant of the Marine Corps, had visited the Khe Sanh Combat Base in January 1968 just prior to our arrival. Hearing his name reminds me of the day when then Lt. General Chapman stopped by the company office during the time Lieutenant Chapman was attending the seven-month instructional course required of all newly commissioned officers. He walked in while I was at my desk one afternoon, pulled up a chair next to mine and asked how his son was doing. In a completely honest appraisal, I told him that his son was performing admirably and showed great promise. He obviously was pleased, thanked me and departed.

Watching all these young Marines in combat — Lieutenants, Privates, Corporals from many different backgrounds — everyone full of life, I marvel at their courage, strength, discipline and willingness to sacrifice their lives in executing orders issued from above. I think of the inevitable certainty that many of these young lives will end prematurely before they are able to fulfill the promise of their birth. Death of the aged is expected,; youthful death is tragic. A parent's worst reality is outliving their children — yet many will have to struggle with that announcement. Every day I survive this war will be a gift.

Chapter 18

KEEP YOUR HEADS DOWN

AS WE BUILD the defensive perimeter around Hill 558, it is necessary to register the fire from our 81mm mortars. Registering fire means you fire several live mortar rounds along the approaches to the defensive perimeter and then note the firing coordinates after desirable impacts. The obvious purpose for this activity is to be prepared at a moment's notice to engage an attacking force. The mortar fire then will help to break up their assault.

During the registering procedure we ensure that the initial rounds impact well beyond our troops. Once you get the range right, you progressively move the impact closer to the front lines. My intention is to register all our mortar fire. I want it as close as possible — up to 25 yards from our position. However, by attempting such precision, I create a potential disaster. Twenty-five yards gives our men very little leeway for error. With one misstep, we could easily drop a mortar round on top of our own troops. With this thought in mind, I put out the word that we will be registering our fire dangerously close to the lines. Therefore, everyone must keep his head down until an "all clear" is signaled.

As we begin dropping rounds into the mortar tubes, I hope and pray that there will be no foul-ups. Then, when we finally drop the impact to within 25 yards, I hear the chilling cry, "Corpsman, Corpsman," following the explosion! We cease fire immediately. I am informed that a Marine has been wounded. My biggest fear jumps to life and my prayers seem unanswered!

He is quickly carried to our medical bunker. I double-time to the bunker to see how badly he is hurt. When I arrive, the doctor is dressing his shoulder. A piece of mortar shrapnel apparently had struck him there. After seeing that he isn't mortally wounded, I begin wondering how he could get hit in the shoulder? Everyone was supposed to have been buttoned up and lying low. I lean over and ask the young man what happened? He replies that he simply was curious about what was going on so he decided to stand up in order to get a better look.

With that confession, I simply lose it! Wounded or not, I can't handle both the disregard for a direct order and the sheer stupidity of the action. I verbally lay into him, chastising him for nearly getting himself killed. The doctor clearly is upset with my lack of sympathy and steps in, asking me to leave while he finishes treating the man.

As I leave, I recall a similar incident between a soldier and General Patton during WWII. The General slapped a soldier, which led to his actions being severely criticized by civilian authorities. He claimed he was reacting to what he had perceived as sheer cowardice on the part of the soldier. I also had just "verbally slapped" a Marine for his stupidity and disobedience. I was furious because someone had almost lost his life because of my decision to be so precise with the mortar fire. As you witness my response to that Marine, what do you think? Do you think I overreacted or would you have done the same thing? Only a complete idiot (or a suicidal) would stand up to get a closer look at incoming mortar fire! Perhaps it was the naiveté of youth and the "it can't happen to me" syndrome.

Chapter 19

ANOTHER DIEN BIEN PHU?

IT IS NOW February 9. About three weeks have passed and several events are beginning to give us cause for concern. The TET offensive is launched throughout all of Vietnam on January 30, 1968 — all except for Khe Sanh. In fact, there is no major activity on the 30th, but things certainly heat up during the next eight days.

The first event occurs on February 2, when apparently 3rd Battalion, 26th Marines (or maybe our E Company on Hill 861A) calls in for an air strike. Our planes bombard the ridge line to our southwest. Two Marine F-4 Phantom jets show up and proceed to make a strafing run of the terrain. As the second jet pulls out of his run, a NVA 50-Caliber machine gun opens up, firing directly into his rear. The plane starts smoking as it circles back toward the base — the pilot hits the silk. Miraculously, the pilot parachutes safely onto the base! I remember thinking what a lucky shot by the NVA, and, concurrently, what a lucky landing by our pilot. When the exact same sequence transpires the next day, I become very concerned. Our "trump card" has always been our Marine close air support. We developed this successful concept during the Banana Wars in Nicaragua.

Then on the night of February 5, the NVA initiates an artillery attack on all our positions. Simultaneously, they launch a major ground assault against Hill 861A. The fighting is incredible. Numerous flares light up the night sky. A roaring cacophony of artillery and small arms fire explodes. The NVA uses pipe bombs to blow some holes in E Company's protective wire. They then proceed to overrun Second Lieutenant Shanley's position. He subsequently pulls his unit back to a supplementary position. With the NVA inside E Company's position, Captain Breeding fires tear gas in an attempt to break up the attack. It has no effect, as the NVA soldiers are drugged. After forcing our lines, the NVA temporarily halts its attack and begins to ransack our gear. With this break, Lieutenant Shanley's men counterattack. One NVA soldier is killed while viewing a *Playboy* centerfold. Another NVA soldier actually jumps on the back of a Marine, while another Marine comes up alongside and stabs his M-16 rifle into the enemy's kidney, and with his weapon on full automatic cuts him in half. Our man is uninjured because he is wearing his flack jacket. This Marine runs away with the upper half of a dead man still hanging on his back, before he finally throws him off. Our Marines now are engaged in gritty hand-to-hand combat. Captain Breeding, a veteran of the Korean War as a young enlisted man, sees one of his Marines come face to face with a North Vietnamese soldier, whereupon the Marine delivers a right cross to the face knocking him to the ground. The Marine jumps on his downed adversary and dispatches him with his K-bar knife. Our Marines use their bayonets, K-bar knives, rifle butts, grenades, fists — anything they can in order to drive the NVA back. Each side engages in this bitter fighting utilizing hand grenades at close quarters—about 10 yards. Fortunately, our Marines are wearing flak jackets. This provides them an advantage since they can lob a grenade, turn their backs, crouch low, and absorb the shrapnel in their flak jackets. Captain Breeding continues to employ more squads in the counterattack. Our bravery and tenacity stun the NVA. Commenting later, Captain Breeding comments, "It was like watching a World War II movie. Charlie didn't know how to cope with it."

Then, as the NVA retreats from E Company's position, we engage them with our heavy 106mm recoilless rifles. We tear them up with a sustained murderous fire. One hundred nine dead NVA soldiers lie both inside and outside the wire. This is a heroic performance by everyone involved in this hellish episode, including mortar support from Captain Dabney's Company on 881S and the 1st Battalion, 13th Marines artillery unit. I'd hate to go up against the U.S. Marine Corps, replete with all our fire-support! The Germans called us "Teufelhunts" in WWI — that is, "Devil Dogs." And don't forget Iwo Jima during WWII: "Uncommon valor was a common virtue."

The NVA regroups around 6 a.m. and conducts yet a second assault. Once again, the tenacity of our E Company Marines, coupled with devastating fire support, blunts this second offensive. The entire area to the north of 861A and 861 is saturated with artillery, air, mortar and recoilless rifle fire. This severely disrupts the enemy's efforts. After the NVA breaks off this second attack, they continue to lob 82mm mortar shells at us throughout the rest of the day.

The whole episode lasts about four hours starting close to 3 a.m. The initial NVA mortar attack alerts everyone on our position, and I look up at Hill 861A, only 1500 meters away, and see the flashes as the rounds burst. More explosions join in from their recoilless rifles and sapper charges. Our flares burst all over the sky above Hill 861A illuminating a large area. They stream down like burning stars leaving a smoky trail behind them. Then, after two or three minutes, each of them extinguishes, only to be replaced by another. The flickering light, the thunder of exploding mortars, artillery and recoilless rifle rounds echo through the hills and valleys. It reminds me of the combat film footage I used to use while teaching Marine Corps History at the Basic School — only this time I'm part of it all! With adrenaline pumping, my primary concern centers on coordinating our efforts in support of our E Company, but I'm totally frustrated since we have no time nor authority to come to their aid. We are on full alert on Hill 558 for a possible NVA attack of our position. Time moves in slow motion and the action continues. Daylight is a welcome sign, and, after the two NVA attacks, the firefight finally subsides, ending with intermittent enemy fire. The NVA has not been successful, thanks to the great defense of Hill 861A. Had they seized that position, the enemy would be looking right down on us and able to inflict serious damage. I keep thinking to myself that should they drive E Company off the hill, we would have to launch an immediate counterattack to regain this key piece of terrain.

Around mid-afternoon we heli-lift replacements to Captain Breeding on 861A to bring him up to strength again. He loses seven men and an additional 35 are wounded. These gruesome statistics always are

PT76 tank (Soviet-built) monument at Lang Vei today

distressing, but the men have done a magnificent job. To be sure, the NVA are around us in force!

The third event doesn't take long to unfold. The NVA, probably still steaming from their February 5 defeat, launches a tank attack against the Special Forces camp at Lang Vei near Laos during the night of February 7 — just a little after midnight. The VC/NVA ,utilizing tanks (PT 76's) for the first time, eventually force their way into the camp.

We hear the opening fire, as someone at the camp furiously fires a 50-caliber machine gun. I never will forget that continuous firing — a chatter, chatter, chatter, which then abruptly stops. All I can gather from the radio traffic is that the 26th Marines are not going to go to their rescue. It is sad because the USMC controls this territory. No Special Forces camp ever has been lost before, so we appear responsible. However, there is evidence that the attack on Lang Vei was intended to draw us out for a major ambush. We don't bite, but it still is a defeat. In any case, it could have been worse.

Higher Headquarters, however, does draw up a plan for a bold rescue to recover the Lang Vei survivors. Several survivors manage to evacuate their bunkers at daybreak and move east to the site of the old

Special Forces camp. A little while later, Marine Air Group (MAG) 36 helicopters, with about a dozen U.S. Special Forces advisors, head for Lang Vei. Lt. Colonel Bill White, CO Marine Observation Squadron 6, commands the Huey gunships. Included in the mission are transport helicopters and escort jet aircraft. As the jets vector in with suppressing fire, the three transport choppers swoop down to pick up the survivors, which include 15 Americans. We witness some of the air activity occurring 7,000 meters to our southwest during this audacious operation.

Many indigenous personnel, mainly Laotians who came across the Vietnamese border earlier, remain after the rescue. They then head east overland toward the KSCB (Khe Sanh Combat Base) and about 3,000 show up requesting asylum on the base. After careful search, they are admitted temporarily for later return to their homeland.

The next event occurs early morning on February 8 around 5 a.m. This time a NVA Battalion launches the first daylight attack in the Khe Sanh area against a 1st Battalion, 9th Marines platoon outpost on Hill 64, some 400 meters west of the battalion defensive perimeter. The enemy supports their attack with mortar and artillery. To gain passage, they blow holes in the barbed wire with pipe bombs and throw heavy blankets on top of the wire. As Lieutenant Shanley did on Hill 861A, Marine Lieutenant Terrance Roach leads a counterattack confronting the NVA attackers in hand combat. Lieutenant Roach is killed in this valiant attempt. The NVA manage to occupy part of Hill 64. Lt. Colonel Mitchell, CO 1/9, commits forces with tank support lead by Captain Henry Radcliffe (another acquaintance of mine) to recover the hill. His counterattack routs the NVA and slaughters them during their withdrawal. We hear the firefight occurring 3,000 meters to our south. Upon termination of the conflict, over 150 NVA soldiers lie dead on the killing field, 1/9 loses 21 KIA (killed in action) and later withdraws the Hill 64 outpost.

Diminished supplies now need replenishment. The C-130 transport aircraft of the Marine Aerial Refueler Transport Squadron 152 accomplishes the major task of transporting support for the base. Other supporting aircraft units include the choppers of MAG 36, MAG 16, the 315th Air Commando Wing flying C-123's, and finally U.S. Air Force 834th Air Division, also utilizing C-130's.

On February 10, an unfortunate event occurs at the base. Enemy fire

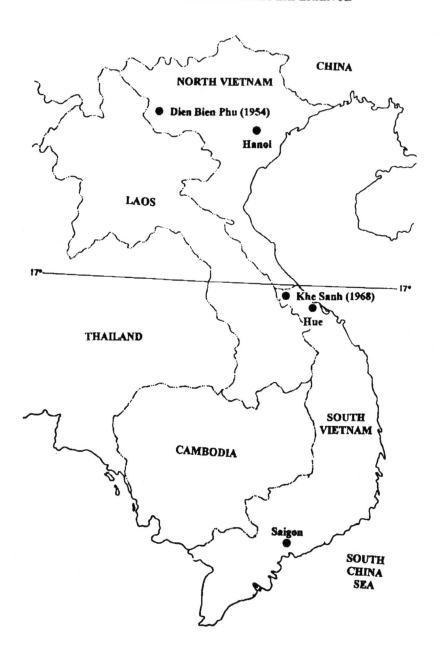

We didn't much care for one of our "intelligence" (?) reports describing Khe Sanh as another Dien Bien Phu possibility.

severely hits a Marine C-130 on its approach to the airfield as it attempts to deliver fuel. Just before landing, the fuel bladders ignite. The aircraft hits the ground, spins around and starts burning. We see the smoke rising from the runway. The pilot and copilot manage to survive, but six other perish. The 1st Marine Air Wing Engineer officer, Lt. Colonel Carl Petersen, USMCR, is among the dead. He had volunteered for active duty a few months prior to this event. This occurrence prompts termination of C-130's landing at the base.

Since the field now is closed, the U.S. Air Force utilizes an innovation devised in 1967 when the airfield was upgraded. The LAPES (Low Altitude Parachute Extraction System) allows aircraft to unload a cargo pellet while never actually landing on the runway. We witness this unique delivery system. The resupply aircraft approaches the KSCB runway with its tail ramp open. As the C-130 glides down the runway about six feet off the ground and reaches its delivery point, the pilot automatically deploys the parachute attached to the cargo pallet on top of rollers. The deployed chute jerks the cargo pallet out of the rear door and it slides to a halt after it hits the runway. The pilot guns the aircraft in an accelerated climb to avoid enemy ground fire. At the same time, base supply personnel dash out to retrieve the needed supplies.

Another unique resupply method is the GPES (Ground Proximity Extraction System), which utilizes a technique similar to an aircraft carrier. An arresting cable is deployed on the ground. With a low altitude approach down the runway, the plot tries to snag the cable with a hook attached to the cargo load. When successful, the cargo is snatched from the rear cargo door gliding to a stop as the Marine Supply personnel rush to retrieve it.

The well thought-out and executed resupply techniques can't fail to impress us. Whenever these techniques cannot be employed, paradrops are utilized. In fact, parachutes deliver most supplies for the combat base. A DZ (Drop Zone) adjacent to the base is designated in a safe area where bundles of cargo can be retrieved. The DZ is about 2,000 meters to our south. I see the C-130 pilots come in at about 600 feet from the east parallel to the KSCB runway. At some designated point, the Marine Air Traffic Control Unit inside the base guiding in the flights gives a signal for the cargo release. The aircraft dips upward and numerous bundles

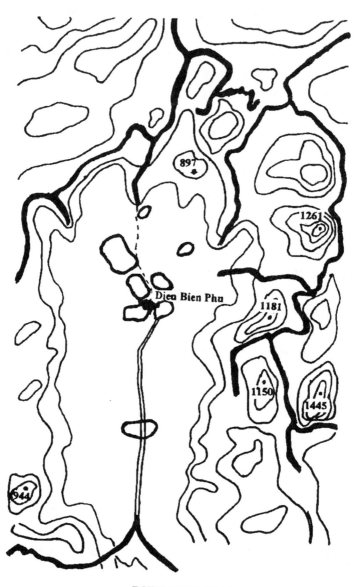

DIEN BIEN PHU

——————— *Viet Minh Roads*   ⬭ *French Defensive Positions*

General Giap holds Hills:
897, 1181, 1150, 1261, 1445, 944

26th Marines held Hills:
881, 861, 861A, 558, 950

spill from the aircraft parachuting to the ground. The deliveries are very accurate with only a few falling outside the safe area. Marines on base fire at these wayward containers hoping to destroy them in order to keep the supplies out of enemy hands. Throughout the siege, we witness approximately 500 paradrops.

It is left to the choppers of MAG 36 and 16 and the C123's of the Army Air Commando Wing 315 to deliver supplies that cannot withstand the violent jolts of LAPBS, GPES or paradrops. These aircraft, carrying medical supplies, special ordnance, other fragile supplies and personnel replacements, dash into the airfield for their deliveries. The more maneuverable choppers and C123's allow rapid approaches and departures. On flights out, they evacuate wounded and end-of-tour personnel. Every "short timer" in Vietnam is "uptight" toward the last days of his tour. With the end so close, no one wants to be that unlucky. Any aircraft's brief stay on the ground attracts enemy fire. I always feel secure knowing these daring and gifted aviators are there to support infantry on the ground. The term Marine Air-Ground Team carries real substance and meaning.

It plainly is impossible to predict what further events will occur, and, at this juncture, I am very concerned. I know you must share my concern! Subsequent to all this activity, we receive a major intelligence report, which I read with great disdain. Consider the fact that in the past two weeks we saw two USMC Phantom aircraft blown out of the sky, we sustained a major attack on Hill 861A, we lost the Special Force Lang Vei Camp, and repulsed a heavy attack near the Combat Base. The report just rambles on about the possibilities of Khe Sanh turning into another defeat, such as the French sustained at Dien Bien Phu!

It is a lousy morale piece, but, more significantly, it is not very comprehensive and insightful. Three major differences distinguish these two events. First, we hold all the significant high ground, while the French were dug into the valley — it was General Giap's forces that then held the high ground. Second, we definitely have more fire support than the French ever had. And, third, we are the U.S. Marine Corps. Throughout my life, I have always wished that reporters, politicians, and others knew more about history. No, this is not going to be another Dien Bien Phu — this clearly is not an acceptable course of action!

Chapter 20

I COULD SURE USE A SHOWER

WE HAVE BEEN IN POSITION now for over two weeks and are under siege. My major task shifts to our living conditions — the health and resupply of the 1,000 plus Marines under our command. Our seasoned NCO's prove invaluable by helping the younger men through the daily drill of an infantryman, but command decisions rest with the Battalion Commander and his Operations Officer. You asked me if I have been apprehensive or even just plain scared while in Vietnam. My answer is that through all of the operations in which I have participated during my months in Vietnam, my responsibilities to the Marines under our command would always suppress my personal anxiety. In truth, I cannot afford the luxury of fear. I have gained knowledge, confidence and superb training over the years — which the men now need. I must do my job — nothing less, and we expect them to do their job as well.

This homemaking health and personal cleanliness task, however, is going to be a real challenge. Human waste always presents the principal concern while in the field, but we had solved that problem long ago. Just take an empty 55-gallon gasoline drum, cut it in half, and put a seat on top. Next all we have to do is ignite some gasoline in order to burn the waste. No, I'm more concerned about cleanliness, since it looks like we could be occupying our position for many months. While there is a river outside our lines and it looks invitingly clear, smaller parties might be ambushed while they are in a compromising state of dress — remember the NVA soldier shaving before our first skirmish.

Unfortunately, the water we have heli-lifted to us supplies only enough for our drinking needs. We require another stroke of luck and a unique solution to our hygiene problem. You might be stumped here unless I give you one additional piece of information. There is a very small — and I mean small — spring bubbling up in a bed of mud in the bowl area formed between Hill 558 and the smaller hill to its rear. Luckily, it is located smack in the middle of our defensive circle. What would you do? Feel free to be creative.

Remember the task organization concept I mentioned earlier? I have a small Engineer Team assigned to the battalion so I call for the team's leader. The team leader, a Sergeant, and I walk down to inspect the small muddy spring. I ask him what he thought would happen if we blew the top off the spring. He replies, "Major, beats me, but let's give it a try." With that we pack plastic "C-4" explosives deep into the mud and run the wires back to the hell box (a box that we crank to generate a spark for the explosives). We yell a loud warning, "Fire in the hole," and then touch off the C-4. The result of this explosion starts with a tremendously muffled thud and then erupts with huge clumps of slimy wet mud thrown skyward landing all over the place. We haven't spared the C-4! After the last clod lands, we rush to our new crater, and, look at that — there are two beautiful rock-lined pools of water. Better yet, they are filling up with water as crystal clear as Perrier! After we finish, the pool complex is over 25 feet long and 15 feet wide.

We drive triangular fence posts, which we normally use for barbed "concertina" wire fences, into each side of the lower pool at a height of about seven feet. Then we tie several more posts across the top, making a platform for four empty 55-gallon drums. The shaved-off drums are thoroughly cleaned and the bases are punctured with numerous holes. This way, we can fill the four drums from the upper pool so that water will stream down on top of us like a household shower. It is large enough to allow four people to shower at once.

All that is left to finish is to devise a shower schedule for all our units. I decide to let one squad (10 to 13 men) shower at a time. It is incredible how great the simple pleasures of life become when they are unavailable! The men can even wash their shorts and socks in the soapy run-off water — an added benefit popular with everyone. What a sight to see Marines crouching around a pool of water — all clad in skivvies washing their dirty laundry. It reminds me of a scene from India where people line the riverbanks of the Ganges River, feverishly washing and rinsing their clothes. During these moments of relaxation, the men often vent energy by engaging in rough water fights and crude jokes. This accomplishment — which we were able to achieve together — will remain a major highlight of my service in the Marine Corps. The benefit of being able to stay clean for over three months enabled us to avoid many of the health problems that plague infantrymen in the field. As I do, don't you feel pride in such an inventive solution to this perennial health problem? Oftentimes we are faced with the need to be creative while living in the field.

Chapter 21

MAJOR, COME QUICK—
THEY'RE DIGGING THROUGH THE HILL!

WE ARE HALFWAY THROUGH February, and you are aware of all the events up until now. The F-4s were downed, a couple of C-130 Transport Aircraft were destroyed on the base runway during resupply missions, Lang Vei was lost, the NVA heavily probed the defensive position of the 1st Battalion, 9th Marines' base, the 37th ARVN Ranger Battalion turned back an attack near the airfield, and Hills 861 and 861A was assaulted in force. And, don't forget that the TET Offensive still is taking place throughout Vietnam.

With all these activities as a backdrop, our Intelligence Officer, Lieutenant Ed Matthews, wakes me excitedly around 1 a.m. with an urgent message, "Major, I think the NVA are digging through Hill 558. I heard them digging!" What next! At first I can't believe what I am hearing. At his request, I get up and go outside to listen firsthand — nothing happens. I try to keep my composure — to be the calm voice of reason — as I assure the young Lieutenant that everything is just fine and it is a rather big hill to even think of digging through. I then go back to sleep — with some difficulty, I might add, because of your loud snoring.

Less than a half an hour passes and once again Lieutenant Matthews wakes me up, this time even more excited. He states very emphatically that they really are digging through the hill and I need to listen again. This time he even manages to disturb your sleep and we are both fully awake.

Khe Sanh Combat Base

*Knoll on south
perimeter
defensive line*

Showers

Landing Zone

C-Rations

Major Kurth on backside of Hill 558

Since he has a rather serious look on his face, I realize he isn't going to leave me alone unless I have another listen. Reluctantly, I arise and slowly walk outside. However, this time it takes less than a minute to hear the noise. And, I'll be damned if it doesn't sound like digging to me as well! We're presented with yet another bizarre situation. Various alternatives and possible reactions race through my mind.

We must not forget to factor in a few vital pieces of information as we consider a course of action. First, when we arrived at our position we uncovered some extensive tunneling in part of the lowland area. When we first started investigating the tunnels, the NVA must have been watching from an adjacent ridgeline, as they lobbed some 82mm mortar shells at us. We stopped investigating since I didn't want a tunnel to collapse on one of our volunteer — yes, volunteer — explorers. Secondly, the NVA had dug under the wire in front of the 1st Battalion, 9th Marines not long ago. And, finally, from history I remembered that the French never expected the German's Armor to pierce the Ardennes Forest and thereby skirt the Maginou Line. One always must look at all possibilities, even if they seem remote. If you study the operations of Israel against their adversaries in the 1967 and 1973 wars, you truly would be amazed because it definitely expands one's thinking about combat—their intelligence operations are legendary. By this time you're a seasoned combat veteran. That being so, what do you think we should do?

My initial reaction is to contain any penetration quickly, so I call out the Headquarters Company Security Unit formed for counterattack operations in the event of a breakthrough. A reserve force is always an essential part of any defensive position. We alert the Security Unit leader and tell him to start forming his men (about 25 Marines) near the base of Hill 558. The digging sound comes from an area about two-thirds of the way up the backside of Hill 558. If they are digging through, they would have started on the north side of the hill in front of our position and then work their way out where we hear the active digging.

In very short order, the Staff Sergeant-in-Charge of the Security Force reports to me. The Marines are locked and loaded and in full battle dress. At present, the sound is somewhat muffled. I discern by the noise that it definitely sounds like a shovel digging into the hillside. The unit fans out, forming a crescent moon shape with their weapons at ready position. We are all tense, as there is practically zero visibility. The command is given to move forward. America's elite fighting Corps is again about to engage the enemy. We move closer and closer — the digging gets louder! I don't know what to expect.

When we finally surround the noise and fire up a couple of flares in order to see more clearly, we find that we actually have captured the largest damn armadillo that I have ever seen! When the armadillo sees the hardened faces of our men glaring down at him, he immediately stops digging and stands fixated. We look at one another with disbelief and eventually start to laugh — partly in awkwardness and somewhat in relief. It is so ridiculous that we decide not to tell the other Marines about our misadventure — it is a shallow victory. Yet, before you pass judgment, you must realize by now how unusual this war really is. The armor plating on that huge Armadillo really did sound like a shovel digging through dirt and rocks. Anyway, we return to camp knowing full well that we are an embarrassing 2 and 0 against the native animal population of Vietnam!

As it turns out, the digging concept is not so farfetched. Though the NVA may not be digging through Hill 558, they are digging all around the Khe Sanh Combat Base. They are even approaching to within 25 to 50 yards from the base's defensive perimeter. They employed this tactic very successfully against the French at Dien Bien Phu. It is the prelude again to the imminent attack we feel is going to be launched against the combat base. Their trenching is so extensive that it is imperative to react quickly.

The NVA even conducts a small unit probe supported by artillery, mortars and recoilless rifles against the 37th ARVN Ranger Battalion early afternoon on February 21. In this instance the NVA does not launch a close-in assault and withdraws by later afternoon. They follow up on February 23 with the most devastating artillery and rocket attack against the base to date. In the space of an eight-hour workday, they pound the base with at least 1,300 incoming rounds and claim ten KIA's and over 50 WIA's.

Just 48 hours following the artillery/rocket attack, the 1st Battalion, 9th Marines experience a regrettable incident. An approximate platoon-size unit conducts a patrol just south of the KSCB in an attempt to neutralize an NVA mortar position that has been firing on the base. The unit is not supposed to venture beyond visual contact with the base, however, the patrol leader somehow loses his bearings. The NVA entices the patrol into an area of elaborate trenches and ambushes it. When the 1st Battalion, 9th Marines Headquarters authorizes a relief patrol, they too are taken under heavy small arms fire. Finally, both Marine patrols are able to break contact and move safely inside the base defense perimeter. We lose eight men KIA during this ill-fated exchange.

On February 27, we implement our new plan. Up until that day, the B-52 Archlight strikes were conducted out at a two-mile radius. We change the next day as we can see the B-52's overhead and bombs beginning to drop—and drop as close as 1,200 meters! The earth trembles, the dirt and trees fly airborne, and a long row of smoke and fire appears to the rear of our position north of the combat base. There is little doubt in our minds that it will serve to disrupt any impending attack against our positions.

I give our higher headquarters high marks for developing this tactic, as only two days later on February 29, an NVA Regiment initiates an assault against the 37th ARVN Battalion near the southeastern perimeter of the combat base. The base 105mm Howitzers, the bigger guns at the Rock Pile east on Highway 9, and air assaults break up this attack. The NVA halt their activities and drift away into the hills. They have had enough. Local inhabitants report a count of around 300 dead NVA—soldiers lying along the eastern approach roads.

Little do we know on March 1 that this will be the last major attack against any position in the Khe Sanh area. However, we now settle down to a daily artillery duel. One exception occurs on March 8 when the ARVN Ranger Battalion conducts a probe east of the airfield and engages their northern countrymen in their trenches. They dispatch 2 dozen NVA. The CO and I receive an intelligence summary in the middle of March from our S-2 Intelligence Officer stating that the mountain tribesmen in the area witness the withdrawal of several sizable NVA units toward Laos. These movements, however, do not cause the cessation of the shelling of our positions and I'm certain there still is a major NVA presence. A major crescendo arrives on March 23 when 1,109 NVA incoming rounds explode on the base.

Chapter 22

WHAT THE HELL WAS THAT?

SINCE THINGS HAVE quieted down a bit and our defensive perimeter is shaping up, I decide to employ two more devastating weapons to aid in our defense. I first learned these weapons back at Quantico, Virginia, when I was an instructor at the Quantico Basic School, a seven-month course for new 2nd Lieutenants. I never thought then that I'd actually utilize the weapons in question.

The first one is actually quite simple. You take a complete roll of barbed wire, which is hollow in the middle, and pack the hollow space with C-4 plastic explosive. Then you mount it on a stake about 2-1/2 feet off the ground. Next, you build a double sandbag wall behind the contraption to protect your own troops. Finally, you just string the detonating wire back to the hell box located amidst our defensive perimeter.

After we set up the first one astride the trail leading through our position, I decide that we need a test to see how effective it will be. After alerting all units in the area and yelling the predictable "Fire in the hole," we touch off the explosives. The result is absolutely amazing! In seconds, detonation transforms two-foot tall grass to a U.S. Masters Augusta, George competition golf course! It lay waste everything within a 180-degree radius — this is unmistakably an awesome weapon. This whole demonstration takes place in the shadow of the high ground to the east and west, and, hopefully the NVA witnesses it. If they are watching from those hills, they will want nothing to do with this.

Anyway, I also have another equally devastating weapon that I want to deploy in the ravines leading into our position—especially towards the west between Hill 558 and 861A—the FOUGASSE! This weapon is constructed using a full 55-gallon drum of jelly gasoline. First you place a full circle of C-4 on the bottom of the drum, then you insert a detonator. By pointing the other end down the ravine and burying the whole thing in the ground, only one end is left uncovered. When the C-4 is detonated, it blows the jelly gasoline, now ignited, out the front and down the ravine. Again, we run the wires back to our defensive position. When we finally have one ready to deploy, it is test time again. Once more, we put out the warning, "Fire in the hole!"

Unfortunately, what I do not see while we detonate this weapon is a Marine helicopter approaching rapidly from behind our position. As it draws near, the gasoline bomb explodes and this huge fireball of flaming napalm shoots down the ravine directly under the approaching chopper! Apparently, it scares the holy hell out of the pilot, since the chopper jerks suddenly to the right, jumps skyward, and then carefully circles back again to land. I head immediately to the landing pad to talk to the pilot. As I arrive, both he and his co-pilot jump out of the aircraft yelling, "What in the hell was that?" They both are visibly agitated. I try to explain and apologize, but only a Marine Infantry officer would comprehend this SNAFU fully. As I speak to the well-groomed pilots, I think to myself, "Welcome to the front line Ground War Aviator!"

The last "confrontation" I had with the Marine air arm was an ice fight at the Subic Bay Officer's Club in the Philippines during the 1961 Laotian Crisis. Of course, we were well into our alcoholic beverages, but these were always friendly confrontations. Every ground officer knows how critically important close air support is to his success and survival. We always know that we really are on the same team. Perhaps we just are envious of their ability to return to their Gun Fighter Club in the rear area for a juicy T-bone steak and cold beer after engagements, while we are stuck eating C-rations for months. The taste of luxury in the rear areas makes me think that maybe I should have been a pilot after all! I say that, but do I mean it? A Marine helicopter aviator friend from Lieutenant days had been shot down five times in Vietnam and managed to survive without capture. This was not without lasting detrimental effect to his nerves, however. Helicopters can be clay pigeons for the enemy.

Chapter 23

OUR RECORD CLIMBS TO 3 AND 0

THE KHE SANH COMBAT BASE is the probable "grand prize" in the eyes of the NVA high command. However, overrunning the base will not bring them total victory. They still have to contend with the entire 1st Battalion, 9th Marines near Hill 64, and our 2nd Battalion, 26th Marines astride the northern approach route. I cannot speak for Lt. Colonel John Mitchell, but I am sure his battalion is prepared to defend its position and uphold the glory of the Corps. What I do know is how well we are prepared to deal with an NVA assault — we will prevail!

The operation plan for the defense of Hill 558 is complete. We have to keep the plan fairly simple and short, as there are no copy machines on our position. We use four pieces of carbon paper in our portable typewriter and hit the keys firmly. This way we have five copies of the plan for our three rifle companies, the Headquarters Company, and for my use in the COC. The basic order is short and concise, "Defend the Hill 558 complex and deny the enemy passage down the Rao Quan River trail toward the Khe Sanh Combat Base."

The more detailed part of the operation plan involves the annexes' need to coordinate our entire effort. The annexes included are for the following: fire support coordination, communication, logistics, intelligence and personnel. Each annex spells out tasks and activities established for each staff section, line unit and supporting units. The planning must be thorough, comprehensive and understandable to all personnel executing its provisions.

The Fire Support Coordination Annex is the most significant, as it sets forth what weapon systems support our battalion, the map coordinates for all registered artillery and mortar fire, and the placement of larger weapons (such as 81mm mortars and 106mm recoilless rifles). It incorporates the large barbed wire grenades on stakes and the FOUGASSE. Every Artillery and Air Forward Observer is identified and their locations noted. Unfortunately, we are too far inland for our superior naval gunfire, but, if not, this is included also.

The Communications Annex includes all lines of communication by wire, all the PRC 25 radios, the communications personnel assigned to every unit, and all the radio frequencies we will utilize. It is imperative that the Forward Observers know the frequencies to communicate with the mortars, artillery and the aircraft. If you can't talk to them, they cannot support you. The need for cross training in this area is obvious considering the high possibility of casualties.

The Logistics Annex deals with resupply, quantity of ammunition, medical support, handling of prisoners of war, etc. Every single Marine knows that 90 per cent of all wounded personnel evacuated by medical chopper back to a field hospital or hospital ship survive. It is our trump card, after esprit and air support. It includes methods of resupply delivery, including helicopter and airdrop.

The Company Commanders work with their Platoon Leaders and Squad Leaders to establish a field of fire for each two-man foxhole, the M-60 machine guns and M-70 grenade launchers. All these fields of fire must be interlocking, include redundancy, and designed to cover every possible approach to our defensive perimeter. We, in effect, create a band of steel and an iron curtain of our own. Each Company Commander has an Artillery and Air Forward Observer to "call in" direct artillery, mortar and close air support. Higher headquarters control the B-52's, but they show up often. The coordination of artillery and air support is tricky because we cannot shoot artillery or mortars as we vector in close air support. We actually could shoot down our own aircraft!

Everyone is briefed thoroughly and knows his job, including assistants in case the primary officer or NCO goes down in battle. Supplementary defensive positions have been dug on the military crest behind Hill 558 in the event a major enemy attack forces us off the small hill to the south of Hill 558. These types of positions pay off handsomely for Company E on Hill 861A. The Reserve Counter Attack Force is organized and prepared to react swiftly. We are ready to receive a major enemy thrust.

The reason it is imperative to teach Marine Corps history to every Marine in the unit is to convey the unbelievable feats of heroism and victory by our predecessors. They need to know of past valors:

- The incredible stand against the Boxers at the Foreign Legation in Peking in 1900.
- The tenacious defense of Bloody Ridge by Colonel "Red Mike" Edson's Raiders on Guadacanal in 1942 during WWII.
- The furious defense of Toktong Pass in Korea by Fox Company, 2nd Battalion, 7th Marines spearheaded by Pfc. Hector Cafferata and Captain Barber. I joined this unit in 1960 — ten years too late.
- The revered and highly decorated heroes such as John Basilone, Dan Daly, Smedly Butler, Louis Wilson, William Barber, Ray Davis, Chesty Puller, plus many, many more. Meeting the last four named Marines in my early career left a lasting impression upon me. These names are idols to all Marines.

All these Marines faced what appeared to be insurmountable odds, yet they prevailed.

As we sit around impatiently awaiting a chessboard move by the NVA, we feel certain we will defeat our adversaries. No sense of gloom or doom or fatalistic attitude is remotely discernible. In addition, the men have been briefed thoroughly on Captain Earl Breeding's tremendous success and tenacity of Hill 861A on February 5. The sentiment among the men is that if E Company can prevail, then they damn well can match or exceed their performance.

It becomes a sort of mind game, the instilling of invincibility and pride. How many self-help books stress the power of positive thinking? After all, the NVA have political officers teaching, or more correctly, indoctrinating their troops. Think of it all as an important pregame locker room inspirational address. Oftentimes the most inspiring and emotional delivery provides the edge. We have 193 years of "edge."

We are so ready and alert that early this morning the troops near the Rao Quan River trail spot some movement to their front. They immediately go on full alert with weapons loaded and locked. As the mist clears, one Marine raises up and fires his rifle. He scores a direct hit and all movement stops. The Marine is fully aware of his purpose and careful in his execution. Now other Marines realize that purpose and are standing down. With that single shot we go up 3 and 0 against the animals of Vietnam— first the monkeys, then the armadillo, and now a Vietnamese deer. Such is life! Pumped up to shoot a deer!

However, this time there is a benefit, as we will eat our kill. Under plenty of cover, two men go out about 100 yards and retrieve the deer. There is little doubt that we can find an experienced deer hunter and dresser in our midst. Thus, the deer is cooked and offered to all. At this point fresh deer meat is superior to C-rations any day of the year and relished by many who previously disliked venison. This whole episode provides comic relief to a strained situation as word spreads around the remaining perimeter. Now, in the interest of a good meal, every man is alert in the search for deer, as well as the enemy.

Chapter 24

THAT'S A B-26!

IT IS NEARING THE END of February, and our overall air activity in the entire Khe Sanh area is intensifying. The C-130's continue to resupply the combat base, but now have instituted a unique delivery system due to enemy artillery and mortar fire. Upon landing, the aircraft keeps moving down the runway with the cargo pallets pushed out the back. Once the cargo is extracted, the plane heads skyward. A moving target is harder to hit, and the speed of the entire operation disrupts the NVA's reaction time.

The B-52's are pounding targets as close as 1,200 meters from our perimeter. You can see the aircraft approach, watch the bombs drop in stacks and slam into the ground. We feel the ground shake and can't help but feel pity for those on the receiving end. I never know how effective these devastating attacks are since we still cannot venture out beyond the defensive perimeter.

The F-4 Phantoms are delivering all types of ordinance — including napalm — within fifty yards of our positions. The hills around us, once beautifully vegetated, now resemble photos from an Apollo moon mission. Then, one clear sunny afternoon, we hear the drone far off of an incoming aircraft. We spot the plane to the southwest as it heads directly toward our position. The Battalion Commander, Lt. Colonel Heath, asks me if I can recognize the aircraft type. I grab a pair of binoculars to get a better look. Since high school, I always was interested in World War II and early jet aircraft. Upon focusing the lens, I am surprised as I yell at Lt. Colonel Heath, "That's a B-26 World War II light bomber and it's all black!"

When the plane is directly overhead, it releases a bunch of small packets about the size of a tea bag that land both on top and in the front of Hill 558. I run to the top of the hill and see some Marines looking around the area and picking up some of these packets. Several Marines are stunned when the packets explode in their hands. They aren't severe enough to dismember or tear off flesh, but they sting and bruise them. We quickly circulate the order to leave them alone.

The real questions now are, "Who delivered them, and why?" The "why" we figure out in short order, since those little packets also explode when you step on them. Therefore, we determine they were dropped to provide us an early warning device along the approaches to Hill 558. And most were dropped on the front side, or enemy side, of the hill. As time wears on, these things become a little more powerful and you cannot pick them up without the possibility of a more severe injury.

The "who" is the true mystery. The only valid chance we have of making a determination is to inquire by message up the chain of command, and, especially to DONG HA DASC (Direct Air Support Center), which controls all aircraft in northern I Corps. We end up drawing a total blank, as no one takes credit or acknowledges the delivery. These mysteries will continue until maybe corroborated one day, but my best guess is CIA involvement, as they utilized B-26's at the Bay of Pigs in 1960.

The mystery leaves me with an odd feeling. What was the big secret? Why not tell us about it?

Chapter 25

AGENT ORANGE

THE AIR ACTIVITY all around the Khe Sanh area continues to unfold. We have seen A-4 and F-4 fighters, B-26 and B-52 bombers, C-130 and C-47 cargo aircraft, and helicopters of all types. However, one other aircraft methodically goes about its business around our positions spraying what we are told is a defoliant. These are C-123 Air Force aircraft often circling our position releasing their spray over much of the beautiful foliage not already destroyed. The purpose of this operation is to kill the dense remaining foliage nearby, thereby exposing the large NVA units surrounding us so we can engage them.

Admiral Elmo R. Zumwalt, Chief of Naval Operations in the U.S., authorized this concept. No one knows at this time that this spray called "Agent Orange" is dangerous or carcinogenic. On a couple of occasions, Captain Dave Caldon, our Air Officer, jokes that we need not take a shower that day since we were being doused by the Air Force!

Once again we have a clandestine and uncoordinated operation unfolding around us, but apparently this concept is not well tested or understood. I never give it another thought or even feel we are the ones in danger, too.

Note: Later the Agent Orange controversy swirls around the halls of Congress. I subsequently have learned that several people who served with me contracted cancer and that cancer incidents among Khe Sanh veterans is abnormally high. Admiral Zumwalt's son, a Navy officer on

Rivereen patrol, died early from cancer — supposedly due to Agent Orange. Congress finally addressed the Agent Orange issue. Public Law 103-446, the Veterans Benefit Improvement Act of 1994, codified presumptions of service connection for certain diseases associated with herbicide exposure in Vietnam that VA had recognized administratively. Conditions recognized as service-connected for Vietnam veterans based on exposure to Agent Orange or other herbicides include the following:

1. Chloracne
2. Non-Hodgkin's lymphoma
3. Soft tissue sarcoma
4. Hodgkin's disease
5. Porphyria cutanea tarda
6. Multiple myeloma

Admiral Elmo R. Zumwalt, Jr.,
USN, Chief of Naval Operations

7. Respiratory cancers (including cancers of the lung, larynx, trachea and bronchus)
8. Prostate cancer
9. Peripheral neuropathy (acute or subacute)

And, Spina bifida condition is recognized in the children of Vietnam Vets.

If the VA finds that the above conditions are service related, then treatment of the ailment is free of charge at the closest VA hospital. Also, they currently authorize the Dependent Indemnity Compensation (DIC) $816 per month to the surviving spouse of the Vietnam veteran.

Chapter 26

THE "SUPER GAGGLE"

YOU KNOW THE FATE of some of our support aircraft shortly after we arrived on position at Khe Sanh. Both fighter and transport aircraft have been destroyed at the combat base or in the skies above. The NVA holds the ridgelines just down from the hills we occupy. They are entrenched on the most prominent ridgeline that extends back from Hills 861 and 861A. From positions on that and other high points, the NVA engage our aircraft and lob mortar shells on our positions at 881S, 861, 861A, 558 and the base itself.

Resupply of our position by conventional means becomes untenable since it takes too long and invites enemy fire. Our outpost on Hill 881S has had dangerous experiences with trying to land choppers — even one at a time. Captain Dabney had occasion to call for a Medivac chopper to evacuate wounded Marines. NVA artillery and mortar fire chased off one chopper prior to completion of its mission and another was razed with machine gun fire making the chopper inoperable. The aircrew temporarily was forced to become infantry personnel. Fortunately, a few did make it in to resupply and evacuate personnel. Because of this dangerous situation, the higher-ups will have to devise a new stratagem for resupplying us. We don't need supplies often, but occasionally it is a necessity. They inform us that they have developed a new approach and we should prepare for resupply at a moment's notice.

What transpires next is one of the most incredible, unique, noisy, speedy and well thought-out strategies I have ever witnessed in my life. For you to be there with me to observe this phenomenon is very fortunate, as you are witnessing a true lesson in American ingenuity. It is called a "Super Gaggle" and unfolds like a lightning strike. The afternoon is quiet, calm, warm and sunny, when all of a sudden the following sequence erupts:

1. Two F-4 or A-4 Marine fighter aircraft come screaming in — flying parallel to the ground on our east and west side with their 20mm cannons opening fire.

2. Following close behind are two more fighters firing furiously and engaging the high ground on our east and west.

3. Immediately behind the second pair of blasting jet fighters fly two additional aircraft billowing thick white smoke from underneath and laying down a huge smoke screen right on top of those high points of ground.

4. The smoke forms two huge white walls as barriers — actually isolating our position from sight.

5. Then a fleet of six to eight helicopters, flying in perilously close formation, appear at one end of the white corridor headed directly for our landing zone. These choppers are in such close proximity that I wonder why their rotor blades never entangle one another. The choppers have supplies slung underneath the aircraft. Smoke lingers on the hillsides as the gaggle of helicopters sweeps into our LZ. In unison, they release their cargo abruptly. The group then swings around quickly and heads out.

Drawing by
Chris Kurth

6. As they depart, two more Marine jet fighters roll in — again cannons blazing — raking the hills with gunfire as the smoke dissipates. As quickly as it starts — it comes to an end.

We convey what supplies we need on Hill 558 by radio message to our Logistics Officer, Captain John Martikke at the KSCB. He is part of the rear echelon 2/26 Headquarters group commanded by Major Royce Bond, our Battalion Executive Officer. However, this group is not a normal "rear echelon" contingent, as the NVA pummels them constantly with incoming fire. I guess there is no real safe haven anywhere in the Khe Sanh area! After the first "Super Gaggle" mission, I share my appreciation on the radio with Captain Martikke and the 26th Marine Regimental HQ.

Although the media routinely portrays the military as inept bunglers — watch any episode of MASH — seldom do the armed forces receive credit for both the brilliant performance and creativity they often display. Being a military person is like being a policeman — no one cares about you until they need you.

Chapter 27

WE HIT THE MOTHER LODE

WE SIT ASTRIDE a trail that comes down alongside the Rao Quan River from the north. The trail is the main avenue of approach from the north to the Khe Sanh Combat Base and the old French plantation. We have patrolled along that trail earlier and would not be surprised if a major thrust against us comes along this route. Therefore, the Division Intelligence people deploy electronic listening devices (introduced via air) that detect movement along portions of the trail. When movement is detected we will vector in attack aircraft against the area.

One evening just prior to midnight, we are informed that the sensors have discovered fairly heavy movement. A couple of F-4 Phantoms are launched in order to drop ordnance on the same area. Shortly afterward we hear the aircraft scream low overhead and drop into the valley. Both aircraft deliver their bombs and depart. We hear all the initial explosions, but then something else begins to happen. There is one, then two, then three, then four, and then many more secondary explosions. To a Marine combat veteran at any level, that means we hit an ammunition dump or a truck caché. The multiple explosions and lightning-like flashes against the dark night sky remind me of childhood 4th of July fireworks — and the beauty of the deadly display awes me.

We happily contact Regimental Headquarters at the Khe Sanh Combat Base with a Situation Report informing them that the air attack has resulted with multiple secondary explosions. It appears that we have hit the mother lode! We are convinced we destroyed at least two NVA ammo cachés. Our Headquarters responds asking us to "Please, wait a minute." We wait more than just one minute! When they ultimately respond, they totally burst our bubble.

It seems the 1st Marine Air Wing is testing a new multi-head bomb. What we are hearing and seeing are many little bombs packed into a bomb warhead, which scatter on impact. Of course, no one ever bothers to tell us about this type of weapon — so we are not uncomfortable about our original analysis. This is just more evidence that competing groups are fighting this war and that coordination with the front-line combat units is woefully inadequate. The refrain continues — why didn't they let us know?

CHAPTER 28

AFTER THE OBVIOUS—
WHAT'S YOUR SECOND CHOICE?

WITH THE ADVENT OF MARCH, we've reached the halfway point of our thirteen-month Vietnam assignment. We have witnessed the bizarre, the humorous, profound sadness, frustration, embarrassment, and, most importantly, we have survived! Will the next six and a half months be a continuation of these events or will they be less adventurous? In my mind, and I guess yours too, the modus operandi probably will continue just as it has. This funky war isn't going away anytime soon and we still need to survive the second half.

However, after having crossed hump day, the first occurrence proves to be one of the most curious events of my tour. The day starts virtually cloudless. The sun is warm, but not intolerable. Since the middle of February, we saw sporadic NVA shelling throughout the area. Yet, this particular day is quiet and serene. I feel we have settled into a stalemate. We are tired of sitting on our butts, simply waiting it out. Some of the troops even put together a touch football game on a makeshift gridiron adjacent to our helo-landing zone. And, as always, they can enjoy a good shower after a hard-fought game. At least no one dies in these battles! In fact, this may provide a valuable insight into the true nature of competitive sports — maybe we need some sort of friendly confrontation to blow off steam?

This is the setting as Lt. Colonel Heath, you and I sit on the south side of Hill 558 basking in the brilliant sunlight, chatting and passing the time. These types of conversations can lead anywhere, but through it all you sense a feeling of loneliness. We all have been separated from our families and loved ones for seven months. It doesn't make it any easier knowing that this is my second thirteen-month unaccompanied tour (first being the Far East from May, 1960 to June, 1961) or that we are defending the so-called "Domino Theory"!

Anyway, the skipper turns to me and asks, "Jerry, if you could have any one thing right here, right now, not counting the obvious, what would it be?" I hesitate for only a brief moment and reply, "Ice cream." As God is my witness, lightning can strike me as I say this if not absolutely true, no sooner do I utter the words "ice cream" that a large H-53 helicopter appears from behind Hill 1015 and 950. It heads our way with a huge cargo net suspended underneath. It moves rapidly toward us, swoops down on our helo-pad, hovers briefly, releases its cargo, and departs even faster than it arrives.

I yell at the Headquarters Company Gunnery Sergeant to take a look, but he already is running in that direction. We are so blessed to have so many professional and dedicated NCO's in our unit. After his cursory inspection, he comes dashing up our way yelling, "I can't believe it — it's ice cream, about 10,000 Dixie cups!" My personal request has been answered — and I mean fulfilled within five seconds of my utterance!

Upon reaching the Dixie cups packed in dry ice, we grab our share. I quickly ingest several Dixie cups pausing only to make the difficult decision between chocolate, vanilla and strawberry. It is a welcomed treat and a most unique C-ration. However, ten minutes later, my stomach tells me that gulping down a large amount of ice cream on an empty stomach after a long abstinence from dairy products isn't a brilliant idea.

After reaching satiation, the obvious question arises. Who sent the gift? I forward a message through Regimental Headquarters at Khe Sanh all the way to 3rd Marine Division Headquarters. Surely the Division G-4 Logistics can supply a ready answer. Several days pass without a concrete response from anyone. We never ever learn what benefactor was responsible and whom we needed to thank. It will remain another of the mysteries of my Vietnam experience. Certainly divine intervention is capable of such perfect timing! We all believe what we want. After the word spreads around camp about my heavenly request, many Marines admonish me for not requesting many more important things on the continuum than ice cream! Yet, even if no one wants credit for the treat or it isn't divine intervention — it is nice for many lonely Marines to be "touched by an angel" one afternoon.

Chapter 29

GOD, HOW COULD YOU LET THAT HAPPEN?

OUR BATTALION is extremely fortunate to have an outstanding Chaplain to administer to our spiritual needs. Each infantry battalion in Vietnam has an assigned Chaplain to provide religious services to the men. The assignments are not done by religious denomination, rather on who is available at the time of a billet opening. Therefore, a unit could have a Methodist, Baptist or Presbyterian minister, a Jewish Rabbi, or Catholic Priest — whoever is due for assignment. They are a special type of religious leader — usually very down-to-earth, realistic and straightforward men, as they would have to be to reach men in wartime circumstances, yet, still very spiritual.

We happen to have a very personable Catholic priest, Father Robert Brett. He identifies with all the men and ministers to them constantly. On Sundays he holds mass on a makeshift altar and attendance is quite good. We obviously have to hold several services so we do not weaken our overall defenses. The large attendance doesn't surprise me, since every man feels threatened and seeks divine guidance and favor. My constant prayer, since even before I arrive in Vietnam, asks the Lord to grant my safe return to my family. I ask that he give me a future with my 1-1/2-year-old son. It will be tragic if he grows up without a father and I already have missed some of his early years. I happen to be Catholic so I attend all of Father's services whenever possible.

Father Bob is totally dedicated to his job and truly wants to be there to watch after his community of men. He walks around our positions on Hill 558 with a small placard on the side of this helmet that says, "Some men wait to the 11th hour to believe, but they die at 10:30!"

On February 5, he demonstrates just how far and at what risk he will go to perform his duties. E Company on Hill 861A is heavily attacked at 3 a.m. suffering numerous casualties. After both of the NVA assaults are repulsed, we know we will have to send replacements via chopper to Captain Breeding. At around 7 a.m., a couple of choppers arrive at 558 to pick up the replacements. One of the people already aboard one of the choppers is David Duncan, a civilian combat photographer, who is the only journalist to ever visit our forward positions at Khe Sanh. His photographs become famous. Just as the last replacements board, Farther Brett runs up to a chopper and tells the pilot he will be accompanying the replacements. He never bothers to ask permission or seek approval; he just feels he is needed on Hill 861A after their ordeal.

When he arrives on the hill, Captain Breeding spots him and blurts out, "Who's that SOB walking around without his weapon?" When told it was the 2/26 Chaplain, he adds, "That's great, I don't need to baby-sit any more people on this hill." That doesn't faze Father Bob; he just continues to talk to as many men as possible. The men are deeply impressed and appreciative of his commitment and presence.

He spots the Marine positions on Hill 861, K Co 3/26 and tells one of the senior NCO's that he wants to visit those men too! He is told that it is impossible, as there is a minefield between the two positions 300 yards apart. The good padre is very serious and insists, so they walk over to Hill 861 trying to avoid the mines. After a brief visit, he returns to 861A and then back to 558 by mid-day. I would not have let him go if he had bothered to tell me of his intentions. In his mind, his desire to be of service and to administer to those men superseded any need to seek permission. Who can argue?

A few days later, he approaches me as I am traversing the perimeter to inform me that he is short of religious supplies. He requests permission to chopper back to the Khe Sanh Combat Base for one day and then return the next with his supplies. He also wishes to touch base with a friend and counterpart at Regiment. I tell him that it is too dangerous to chance the trip and besides he had tempted fate once already. I ask him

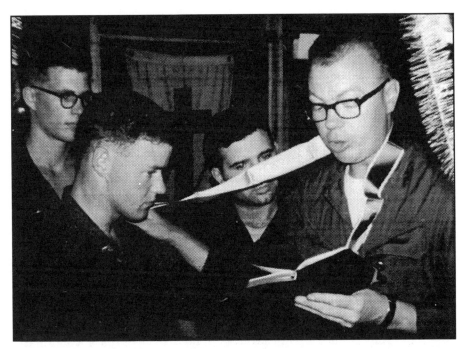

Father Robert Brett, Chaplain for the 2nd Battalion , 26th Marines, attends to the spiritual needs of the men aboard the Hue/Phu Bai Combat Base in Vietnam.

to do the best he can with what supplies he has left.

Within a week Father returns with another request for a chopper trip back to the base. He tells me he has a job to do, just as I do, and he can't do it properly without the requisite supplies. What is your call? Should you let him go back to serious danger? His sincerity and impassioned plea are too much for me — I call for the helicopter.

He departs our position with no interruption and arrives quickly at the base. I make further arrangements for his return the next day. My gut feeling is that a man of the cloth surely would be granted special protection.

The next day a chopper arrives at the combat base runway to pick up Father Brett, his enlisted assistant, Corporal Alexander Chin, and a few other individuals. As they approach the chopper, the NVA begins shelling the base with 122mm rockets. Father Brett tells another Marine to take his place aboard the aircraft, and he and Chin run back to a trench alongside the airfield. The helicopter lifts off headed for our position.

The shelling continues and one rocket round finds the trench immediately killing several Marines. Among the dead are Father Brett and Corporal Chin. The Corporal, an African/Chinese American, already possesses two purple hearts for wounds previously sustained. He also had been one of my S-3 jeep drivers during our operations in the Hue/Phu Bai TAOR.

I cannot express adequately my shock and regret when I receive the message informing me that Father Brett and Corporal Chin had been killed in the rocket attack just moments ago. At this point I'm not sure about your total reaction, but let me assure you it immediately changes my attitude and belief in divine intervention and/or involvement. How can a merciful God allow this kind of tragedy to a man of the cloth — a good man, a dedicated minister to his people? How do you deal with such an obvious inconsistency? It took me awhile following this event to return to a religious posture, and, I still can't purge it from my mind. I also deal with the guilt that if I had allowed him to go the day of his first request or not at all — he would not have been at that locale on the day he was killed. The total shock extends to every Marine who knew him.

Man's nature is to search for reason, yet he is incapable of answering the big questions and must rely on faith — not understanding. When we become too self-important and think we should know all the answers — all we need to do is sit in the field and gaze at the multitude of stars and planets in the night sky in just this galaxy alone. We then realize how small we are in the grand scheme. Without faith — we become even more insignificant.

Shortly after this tragic loss, I prepare an award recommendation for the Legion of Merit medal. Lt. Colonel Heath signs the correspondence and forwards it up the chain of command to 3rd Mar Div HQ. Father Brett is awarded posthumously that medal. Small compensation, but extremely well deserved. If anyone deserves burial at Arlington Cemetery, it is Father Brett.

Chapter 30

ONE OF THE GREATEST COMEBACKS
I'VE EVER HEARD

WHILE WE ARE OPERATING in the Hue/PhuBai TAOR area, one of our Company Commanders is shot through the fleshy part of his rear end. It could have been a paralyzing wound, but, thankfully, it isn't. Nevertheless, they evacuate him to a hospital somewhere in the south. He mends there for approximately three months before rejoining our unit.

In his travels back he stops in DaNang, which is the operating area of the First Marine Division. With an overnight layover prior to catching transportation north, he elects to visit the Stone Elephant Officers' Club for a few shooters. In short time, a Marine Major walks up to him and informs him that he will have to leave the bar! A quick take by the Captain reveals that the confrontational officer is in starched utilities with defined creases in the trousers and spit-shined combat boots. He asks the Major why.

The Major responds, "Look at you — your utility jacket does not match your utility trousers. They are both wrinkled and unstarched and your boots aren't spit-shined!" The Major is correct in his analysis about the mismatch of the utility jacket and trousers. The Captain was issued new utility trousers because the ones he wore to the hospital were blood-stained and ripped by bullet holes. However, they didn't give him a new jacket. Since he is transient, he never has the opportunity to launder and starch his utilities. Besides, we have no starching facilities along the front lines to perpetuate this perfection! I don't even need to comment about spit-shining boots.

Immediately following the Major's commentary, the Captain asks, "Major, did you serve in the Korean War?" The Major snaps back, "No, I didn't." The Captain calmly responds, "That's two wars you've missed, Major!" With that he quickly retreats out of the club.

This event points out the dichotomy of those living quite comfortably in the rear areas and those in the hinterland slugging it out with Charlie. Ironically, no one prohibits my Marines from going on patrol in the bush even though the knees are torn out of their utilities and their jackets are ripped and stained!

Chapter 31

KHE SANH MAIL CALL

AS YOU MIGHT EXPECT, the mailman isn't too consistent in delivery during our time at Khe Sanh. With NVA gunners loving to take potshots at any aircraft that approach our area, helicopters rarely land, and the choppers are responsible for delivering mail to our troops on Hill 558. Therefore, when there is a rare delivery, it really perks up the men. Well —maybe only those who receive mail. I once received a letter from my wife that took over 30 days to reach me from the canceled postmark.

On one occasion a large mailbag is included in a "Super Gaggle" delivery. I am fortunate to receive several pieces of mail and quickly go to a remote area to read so I might reflect in silence.

One of the letters is from a friend, Cliff Jensen, a former Air Force officer. Our families met in Morocco in 1963 and we became lifelong friends. The letter is in a 5" x 7' brown envelope mailed from Miami, Florida. I open the envelope and find a colored photograph placed inside the letter (see next page). Upon turning it over, I burst out laughing. It provides me with one of those lighthearted moments one needs during our entire Khe Sanh stay. You see — it is a picture of Cliff floating on an inflated chair in his swimming pool with a mixed drink held high in one hand and waving with the other. On the back of the photograph he has written, "Thank God you're over there stemming the "Red Tide" so we can enjoy the American way of life! Thank you from all of us on the home front." Isn't it super having such loyal and devoted friends!

Salute from the home front!

Another letter is an offer through the U.S. Military Post Exchange System for the purchase of an automobile at extremely low prices. At first glance I dismiss it as junk mail, but, having nothing else to do, continue to read. After several moments I break out in a smile again. I am feeling sorry for myself and think maybe I can lift my spirits if I order a Mercedes Benz! All I need to do is fill out the enclosed application indicating model, color, interior colors, tires, etc. That with a $400 check payable to Daimler-Benz and mailed to Germany via the Exchange would conclude the order. I break out my checkbook — after all, I'm not spending a penny during my stay at Khe Sanh. I write the check, include the completed application and give it to the Supply Sergeant for mailing. That is the last thought I give to the matter until it resurfaces.

Chapter 32

WHY THE HELL DID I VOLUNTEER?

THE MONTH OF MARCH 1968 is winding down and I expect that we eventually will be leaving our homestead around Hill 558. As we survey our situation, there is one major thorn in our paw — what to do about the ordnance we have stockpiled consisting of 81mm mortar and 106mm recoilless rifle rounds that have misfired. We keep them segregated, not knowing really how volatile they are. We do not want to leave that danger behind when we leave. It would endanger future U.S. military operations and be a real hazard to any Vietnamese civilians working in the area after the conflict.

We ponder the problem for some time. One solution we feel is unavailable would be to attempt to transport them by air or ground means—they are too unstable. Our final solution is to detonate them in a remote area. Three problems remain: First, how to move them to a remote area. Second, how will we detonate them? And, third, who will perform the job? Because I had ordnance training, I told the CO that I would volunteer to perform the task. I really want to ensure that it is done properly. I remember early on in my Marine Corps career being told by some sage, "Never volunteer." I advance my services as a volunteer before a thorough analysis! I don't expect you to come with me on this duty. In retrospect, I'm doubting my own sanity.

My plan is to load all the misfired ordnance on a mechanical mule (small four-wheel all terrain platform), then drive it out in front of our southern perimeter detonating it well away from the troops. I remember that the NVA had used M-76 tracked vehicles at Lang Vei. So, I will plant the unspent rounds on a line a few feet underground, pack them with C-4 plastic explosives in holes, and detonate. It will make one sweet elongated tank trap. While I am moving the ordnance on the mule alone, it keeps flashing through my mind how ridiculous my situation is and that I am tempting fate. I bounce down a path through our position and out onto the flat ground to our south. All the Marines stand well back as I run the gauntlet. However, I do get help digging the necessary holes. The engineers with us at Khe Sanh help pack some of the C-4 and run the wires to the hell box. I learn, however, that the wires don't run as far away as I desire. I am actually too close in proximity to the buried ordnance. Since I don't know this, I simply lie down on the ground and squeeze the hell box.

What an incredible bang! The C-4 causes the sympathetic detonation of all the unspent rounds. Over a ton of dirt lifts skyward and disperses all over the area. The ground shutters at our position and we practically are buried alive by the falling dirt. We are way too close! However, this explosion disposes of our problem with the ordnance, and we have dug ourselves one sweet tank trap. The last thing I do is to thank our Maker for letting me tempt fate in this cavalier way and still survive. Thanks again!

Chapter 33

WE FINALLY GET ANOTHER CHANCE

AS WE ENTER the last week of March, higher HQ authorizes patrol activity outside our defensive perimeters. On March 24, the 1st Battalion, 9th Marines launches a patrol to their northwest and attacks a dug-in NVA unit about 1,500 meters from their perimeter. Their engagement takes place about the same distance due south of our southernmost position. We are prepared to join the fight if asked, as our butts are getting sore. After a brief firefight, the 1st Battalion dislodges the NVA and returns to its defensive perimeter.

Then, on March 30, the 1st Battalion, 26th Marines gains its revenge for the setback on February 25 when they launch a very well-planned assault against the old NVA ambush trenches. Reminiscent of our sneak attack on January 20, B Company, commanded by Captain Ken Pipes, moves into an assault position under the cover of fog. They call in a pre-assault artillery bombardment and on command the infantrymen launch an assault as soon as the fog lifts. They too catch the NVA off guard with a tenacious bayonet attack, a rare occurrence in the Vietnam conflict to date. Following this spirited and emotional attack, 115 enemy soldiers lie slain on the battlefield. The NVA should have known we'd return with a vengeance to reclaim our fallen comrades — this is the tradition of the Corps. The entire operation is professionally planned and flawlessly executed. The 1/26 S-3 Operations Officer, my counterpart, Major Charlie Davis, did most of the planning and Captain Pipes is awarded

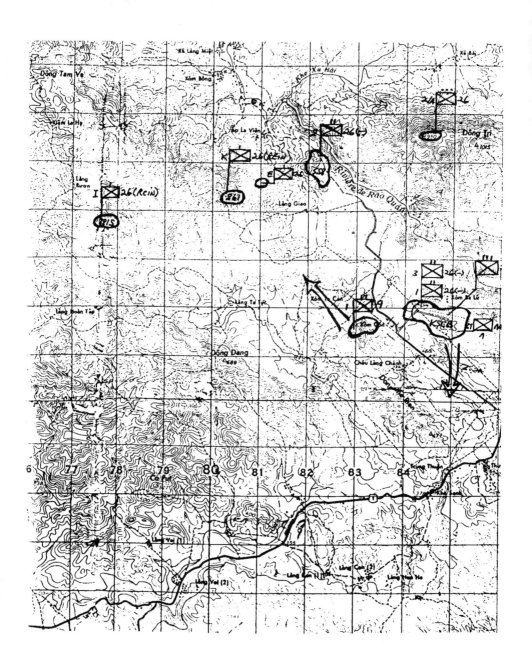

Offensive actions conducted
on March 24 (1/9) and March 30 (1/26)

the Silver Star medal for his conduct during the operation. I know so many fellow officers at Khe Sanh — it is an excellent group.

There isn't much to celebrate on April Fools' Day, as any attempt at humor seems wasted. It does, however, mark the end of yet another month of our tour — the end seems much closer now. I have been the S-3 Operations Officer for seven months and begin asking about reassignment as a Battalion XO, or even Battalion Commander. The latter is a remote possibility, since that billet is coveted by many Lieutenant Colonels already in the country or those who have just arrived. I speak with the CO, Lt. Colonel Heath, and he suggests that I contact the Division G-1 (Personnel) Officer in Quang Tri. I do so and am now on record for reassignment.

It also marks D-Day for Operation PEGASUS with the missions of relieving the Khe Sanh Combat Base, opening Route 9 to Khe Sanh from the east, and destroying the NVA units. A new Provisional Corps Vietnam (PCV) is established with Lt. General Rosson, USA in command to conduct Operation PEGASUS. PCV is placed under the operational control of Marine General Robert Cushman, Commanding General, III Marine Amphibious Force. We receive a message informing us of the new operation.

The 1st Marine Regiment is transferred to an area near Camp Carroll with the mission of initiating the opening assault to the west along Route 9. On April 1, they capture key objectives on both sides of Route 9. The 1st Air Cavalry Division, US Army continues the attack toward Khe Sanh in a series of helicopter assaults. I learn that on April 3 the Army units are 6,000 meters east of the base. We can begin to see the Huey attack aircraft engage the enemy to our southeast.

The 1st Battalion, 9th Marines (now commanded by Lt. Colonel John Cahill) join the attack by moving against and seizing Hill 471 due south of the base about 2,000 meters. They manage to stave off a major counterattack by elements of the "infamous" 304th NVA Division and deal them a crushing defeat. With that offensive operation, we terminate the siege! I quickly finalize plans for our first offensive action since January 20. A real sense of excitement prevails as word goes out to our companies that we are gearing up for action. Everyone is fed up with inaction and punishment from the surrounding enemy. I know we are ratcheting

Captain Matthew P. Caulfield
S-3, 3/26

Captain William H. Dabney
CO, COI, 3/26

Major Joseph M. Loughran
XO, 3/26

Captain Charles E. Davis III
XO, S-3, 1/26

Captain Edward M. Ringley, Jr.
S-3, 1/9

We were all graduates of amphibious Warfare School, Quantico, VA, Class 2/67, and ended up sharing the siege at Khe Sanh in key billets.

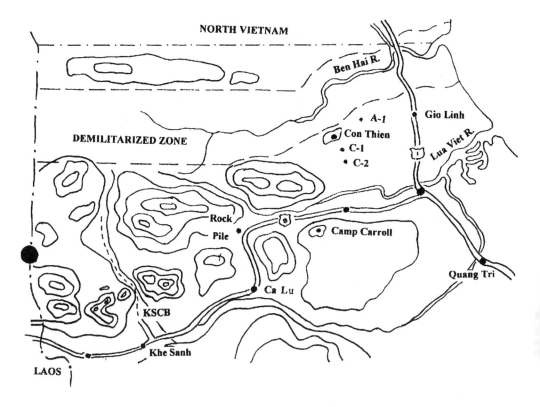

up to greater danger with this upcoming offensive action. The media has been scaring our families at home with hype throughout the entire Khe Sanh engagement.

Since it now appears that the massive enemy threat in the area has dissipated and the siege is officially over, we receive permission to once again send out combat patrols. The initial company-sized patrol is aimed at checking out the ridgeline that overlooks our position on the west— that is, to the rear of Hills 861 and 861A. The patrol will depart at sunrise on April 6, as they don't have far to travel to reach the base of the hill. We also can offer direct line-of-sight fire support. Just prior to departure, Captain Dave Caldon, Battalion Air Officer, asks me if it would be okay for him to join the patrol, since he is bored sitting inside the perimeter for a long time. There isn't any harm with his request so I let him go. However, it is to be a special day for David.

The lead elements of the patrol reach the military crest of the ridgeline (an area just below the topographical crest utilized for defensive positions) when they come under intense enemy fire. A few Marines are immediately killed. The patrol returns fire and attempts an assault to no avail. Again, a few more men go down, both wounded and killed. We have a full-blown firefight on our hands. It is obvious that the NVA has not evacuated the area and will defend their positions with vigor.

Fearing any further difficulties, I order the Company Commander to retrieve the dead and wounded and fall back. He has a multitude of things going on simultaneously and seems somewhat hesitant and uncertain. I instruct him to hand the radio to Captain Caldon quickly. When Dave comes up on the net, I tell him to get some air support pronto, as well as to grab the Artillery Forward Observer prior to their arrival, and to pound the area until the close support aircraft finally can blast them. He performs flawlessly with immediate artillery fire followed by the work-horse of our air ground support — the F-4 Phantom. When we finally conclude the operation; however, we have been bloodied so we will be back. David's performance ultimately brings him a Silver Star medal — richly deserved.

While I prepare the final situation report following our engagement, I take time to scan the casualty list. Halfway through the list I can't believe my eyes. One particular name jumps out at me—one of the KIA's (killed in action). The name is very familiar to me because just two days prior to the company's patrol I had conducted a Summary Court Martial of this Marine. He was charged by a superior NCO of physical assault and insubordination. The NCO was riding him pretty hard and he took exception. We were all unnerved to a degree — some more than others. The young man's frustration boiled over and he struck the NCO. This, of course, is an absolute breech of discipline and needs serious address immediately. The military cannot operate successfully without complete, unquestioning discipline; it cannot allow for an individual's loss of control. The Battalion Commander remanded him to a Summary Court Martial, which he directed me to conduct.

The only justification for disobedience is an illegal order. Each individual must determine the morality of a legal order and whether they can execute its provision. The Nuremberg trials in Nuremberg, Germany after World War II judged that people will be held accountable for executing immoral legal orders from above.

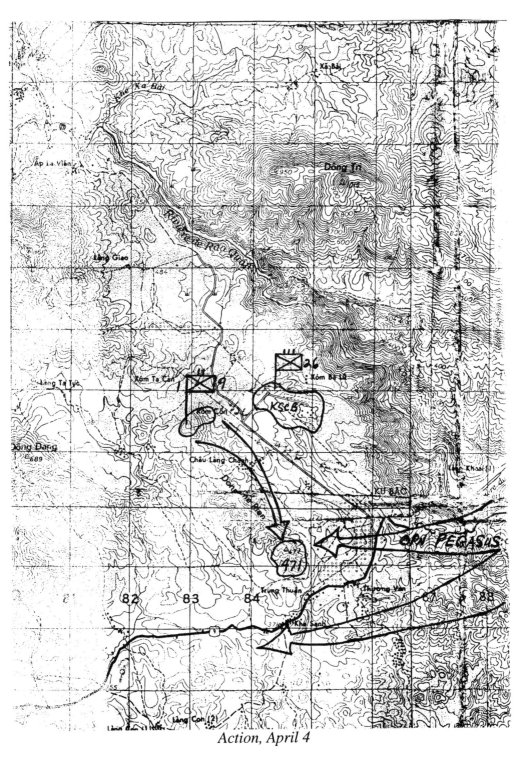

Action, April 4

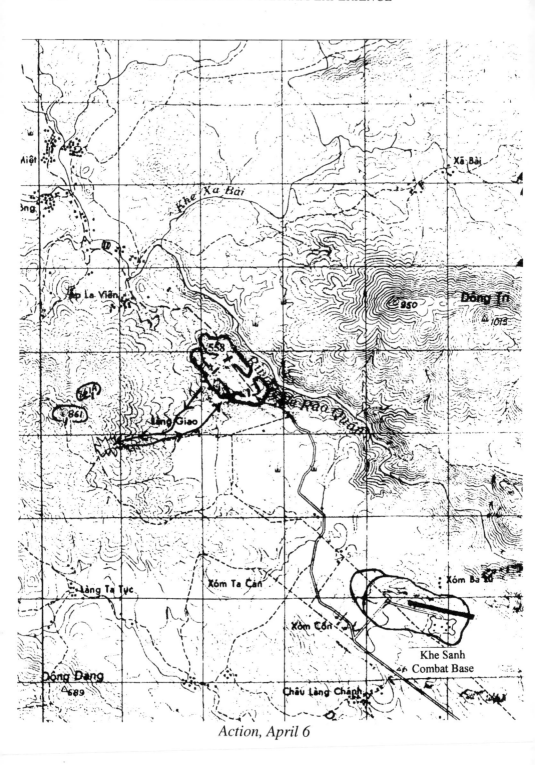

Action, April 6

There are three types of court martials. The most serious is a General Court-Martial. Remember General Billy Mitchell's General Court-Martial in 1925 for accusing the War and Navy Departments of "incompetency, criminal negligence and almost treasonal administration of the National Defense." Ironically, in 1948 he was posthumously awarded a special medal in his honor. Next is a Special Court-Martial with which I am imminently familiar. While commanding one of the Marine Barracks Kenitra, Morocco Guard Companies, I was one of three officers who presided over the trial of U.S. servicemen who had participated in a radical Moroccan movement to overthrow King Hassan in 1964. A Summary Court-Martial is the least severe and applicable in this situation.

1st Lieutenant Jerry Kurth commanding a Marine Barracks Guard Company, Kenitra, Morocco, saluting King Hassan II of Morocco upon his arrival at NAS, Kenitra, Morocco, from U.S. visit. On the king's left is his brother, Prince Moulay Abdallah. Captain Robert Cox, USN, CO NAS, Kenitra, is just behind the prince. (Official U.S. Navy photograph)

The young man, the NCO and a witness arrive in my crude office in the COC. Each in turn makes an official statement and it is left to me to render a verdict. I find the Marine guilty and impose a fine and reduction in rank from Lance Corporal to Private. They all leave the COC and go back to their unit. When the patrol heads out two days later, each man is once again doing his job. The newly punished Marine does not hesitate to go up the hill and execute the assault order given by his Platoon Commander. He is killed attempting to overrun an NVA machine gun position on April 6. So ends his life. In reflection, I wish I never had to punish a man hours before his death. The whole situation seems incongruous and unreal. However, in the end it verifies our esprit and discipline.

Two days later on April 8, we return to finish the job. Our mission is to drive them off the entire ridgeline. I want in on this one, since we were so badly hurt before. The plan calls for the assault force, F Company (Reinf) to depart our position on Hill 558 at 4 a.m. as that gives us two hours to reach our line of departure (LD) for the attack. Prior to our departure, we must perform a myriad of things in preparation. Of course we alert our E Company that we are coming, as we will pass fairly close to their position and don't want them to mistake us for an enemy unit if heard or seen. Getting the men ready is tedious too since we need to soundproof every Marine. We can't have any clanging of dog tags, canteens, K-bars or weapons and tape everything together or tape light items to something more solid. We put socks over our rifle butts to deaden any contact. Men from Companies H and G partially fill the vacated positions on the perimeter defense.

The route we take is carefully briefed down to each Platoon Leader. Since we are moving in darkness, we will not put out flank guards very far since too many columns moving in foliage makes far more noise. I feel very comfortable moving at night as I've participated in numerous night training exercises at Quantico, VA, Camp Pendleton, CA, the Zamballes area in the Philippines, and Mt. Fujui in Japan. You always have your compass and often the North Star to help you navigate. Since the enemy can't see us, we avert mortar and artillery attacks. We want to promote two major things. First is stealth — we move very deliberately and silently. Second, it helps immensely if we somehow can mask our movement with a secondary attack of artillery, mortars or other means.

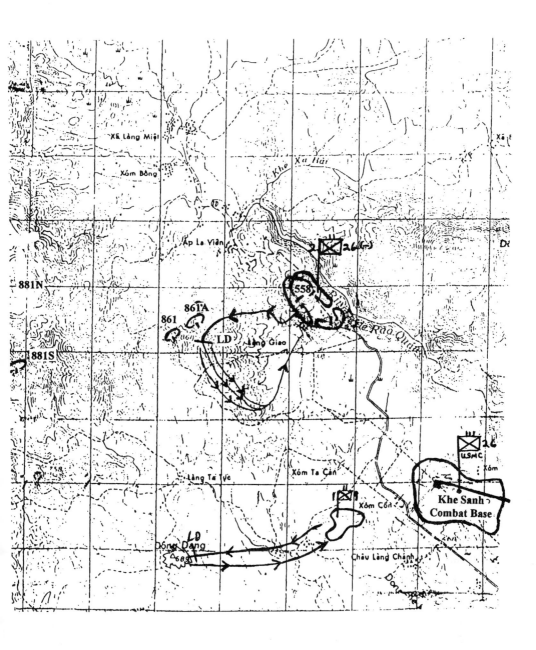

Action, April 8

We choose "Puff the Magic Dragon" to help divert the attention of the NVA from our movement. Puff, as it's called affectionately, is a C-47 cargo aircraft with a rapid-fire machine gun mounted on its side door. The aircraft releases a ribbon of lead against the NVA ground positions as it circles the area. Every fourth round is a tracer round that lights up when fired — appearing as a stream of fire coming from a dragon's mouth. It sounds weird when it fires — a sound I never can duplicate, but never will forget — a unique and uncanny weapon.

As we slip quietly from our defensive perimeter, we descend into the narrow, steep-sided valley about 200 meters directly east of Hill 558. We are thankful that it is a cool evening with virtually no breeze or cloud cover. The terrain features are very discernible allowing easier navigation through the foliage. When it's my turn to step outside our defensive position I feel like I've broken restriction and been freed! Eighty consecutive days inside a barbed wire enclosure has that effect.

At the bottom of the rocky and densely foliaged ravine, I look up to the top of the Hill 861 ridgeline silhouetted against the star-studded sky. It appears to be a formidable climb. I easily can identify individuals close by and our location. Since the ridgeline is due east, it is impossible to get lost. The major task now is to ensure that our advance scouts and the point of our elongated column find a navigable route following our predesignated course as closely as possible. Unit leaders at all levels — fire team, squad and platoon — utilize arm and hand signals to convey directions and orders. We have a long way to go and limited time. If we stray from our planned route, we will not be in position to launch our early morning attack. It is quintessential that we achieve the element of surprise.

Once we come up the east side of the ravine, we move parallel to it for approximately 300 meters before we start our ascent to the Hill 861 complex. "Puff" is doing a magnificent job obscuring any noise we make as it repeatedly circles the top of the ridgeline spuming out its deadly fire. We welcome its strange assuring noise. I'm certain the NVA soldiers are buttoned up to protect themselves against the skydragon.

Progress through the trees and dense underbrush is painstakingly slow. We must pay attention to each branch we touch, each step we take, and how close we are to one another. To avoid the noise and sting of branches snapping back on the person behind, we pass the heavier branches from man to man. Someone inadvertently coughs and everyone stops immediately — frozen at the ready to see whether the NVA has detected us and will punish our blunder with deadly bombardment. The task becomes more difficult as we begin to climb the mountainside to the top of the ridgeline 1,000 meters away. Our flack jackets weigh 15 pounds and don't make it any easier — yet, make no mistake, we are happy to wear them. Vegetation thins and we become better targets.

Finally, we reach our LD (Line of Departure), which is the location from which we will initiate our attack at sunrise just behind the Hill 861 and Hill 861A positions. The LD is below the ridgeline so that the enemy will not see our bodies silhouetted against the skyline. We pause only long enough for the three attacking platoons to deploy on line. As the sun begins to creep over the horizon, the Company Commander, Captain Chuck Divelbiss, gives the command for the attack via radio to his platoon commanders. They simultaneously relay the arm signal to the squad leaders. Over 100 veteran Marines jump to their feet and explode across the ridgeline. A fourth platoon is held in reserve. What a sight! Marine squads attacking like the cavalry of the Old West. At the very moment the attack begins, a wave of excitement and adrenaline

Drawing by Chris Kurth

washes through my body totally immersing me. The sense of impending danger and death is the variable ingredient that heightens the sensation, yet the immediacy of the moment washes away any fear. We catch the NVA by surprise and overwhelm them by the size of the attack. Initially, the squads alternate rushes with one squad on the ground in a prone position offering a base of suppression fire, while the other two move forward. It's basic infantry tactics. However, our surprise is so complete that all units stay on their feet continuing their forward momentum. The only thing missing is the sound of the Marine Corps Hymn resounding over the battlefield. One of the men next to Captain Divelbiss goes down with a wound from enemy return fire. The NVA, however, doesn't stand a chance. We sweep over them dropping one enemy soldier after another. Several are caught in their bunkers and die when passing Marines drop grenades into their midst. F Company relentlessly pushes down the ridgeline until all opposition melts away. Victory—and with very few casualties.

As I cross the terrain behind F Company, I see the remains of several NVA soldiers and the bunkers that they occupied throughout the three-month siege. I look over at Hill 558 and can see practically all our positions. They must have watched us shower with envy and enjoyed all those touch football games. It feels great breaking out of our 558 cocoon. As my gaze wanders back to the north and west, I feel like I'm gazing at the surface of the moon. The aerial assault and artillery barrages have laid barren most areas around our defensive positions. The green, lush and plentiful foliage is disintegrated. What was once quite beautiful and serene is no more. We have dropped more ordnance at the Battle of Khe Sanh than any other battle in the history of warfare! Somehow, in a strange way, it is an honor to be part of this piece of history. This will be our last opportunity to take the action to the enemy in the Khe Sanh area. We have received orders to prepare for evacuation to Camp Carroll on April 18.

Just prior to our departure, the new Commanding Officer of the 26th Marines, Colonel Bruce Meyers, who relieves Colonel David Lownds, visits our position on Hill 558 on April 12. On April 14, Easter Sunday, the 3rd Battalion, 26th Marines (not commanded by Lt. Colonel John Studt) initiates the final combat action during the Battle of Khe Sanh.

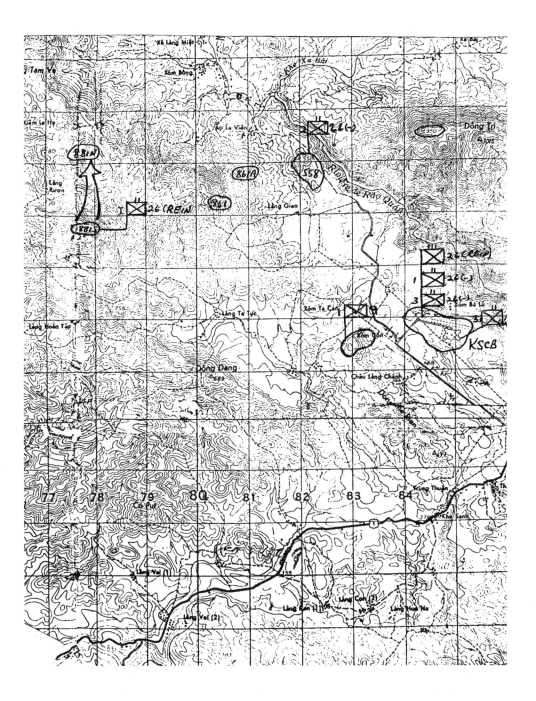

Action, April 14
Last Offensive Action — Khe Sanh siege ends

Sneaking off Hill 881S in darkness, the assault forces launch a devastating attack against Hill 881N at first daylight that sweeps away all NVA resistance. Operation PEGASUS ends on April 15—a date that normally strikes anxiety in us for another reason—the income tax filing deadline date. This is the least of our concerns at this time. The Khe Sanh siege is now history.

Chapter 34

DIG OUT THE MINES

WE HAVE RECEIVED WORD of our Khe Sanh departure and are fresh off an offensive victory. Camp Carroll is our destination with an April 18 departure date. However, another thorny problem needs to be remedied with this impending move. In setting up our defensive position, we installed a couple of minefields. We drew the obligatory minefield map, laying out each mine location with copies forwarded up the chain of command. We query Regiment for guidance about what they think we should do about the minefield. Their reply is very succinct, "Dig out the mines." I have some serious doubts, but an order is an order. How does this sit with you? Do you see any problems? Mines are always problems!

The units that installed the mines will use their minefield maps to dig them up. The minefield maps prepared upon initial installation lay out the position of each mine, distance between each mine, and distance from the edges of the overall minefield. These directions should allow for orderly and safe clearance. However, I worry about this operation from the "get-go." We are endangering the safety and lives of our Marines. The SOP (Standing Operational Procedure) for removing mines is the bayonet probe. The mine clearance personnel approach the minefield at one end assuming a crouching position on their knees. As they begin the clearance procedure they carefully thrust their bayonet into the ground at a 45-degree angle. In so doing, the knife should strike a mine on the side, thereby avoiding the detonating plate on top of the mines and preventing an explosion. Once located, the mine will be removed or maybe blown in place. As I watch the Marines enter the first field, I clearly see the worry on their young faces. They wipe the perspiration from their foreheads and move very slowly. Every one of these men knows the extreme danger and only disciplined military personnel will execute such a mission without bulking. In their hearts, they know this is a calculated risk. How I hate giving such a ludicrous order to our men.

Just after we commence the operation I am called back to the COC bunker for a message. The men aren't in the field fifteen minutes, when that dreaded sound occurs — an explosion! A Marine steps on a mine prior to assuming the crouching position. Part of his foot is torn off — yet another leg casualty. He is evacuated immediately via chopper.

We sent a Sit Rep up the chain informing them of the casualty sustained during the clearing procedure. I've had enough and don't want to continue — I didn't want to start! Once again we ask instructions. You probably guess the reply — remove the mines! We continue the removal operation, although this time with even more severe trepidation. A warning goes out to the Marines in the field to proceed with great caution—as if we need to tell them that! My heart almost stops when there is another explosion—and, another serious leg injury! He too is evacuated quickly. This is the fourth Marine we have lost due to a severe leg injury.

Now the CO and I are extremely agitated and we send a strong message recommending that we suspend this absurd operation. Regiment finally concurs. I believe their future plan is to neutralize the mines with a B-52 strike after the position is vacated. It indeed is deplorable that two young men suffered such crippling injuries prior to this much safer solution! It should be abundantly clear by now that ground troops pay the ultimate price for any decision from above. I always am cognizant of this awesome responsibility every time I recommend or made a decision for the men under our care.

However, the poor leadership of our forces all starts with the arrogant and incorrect decision by President Lyndon Johnson to get involved in another land war in Asia. Once he made such a brash decision, he should have allowed the military to draft a plan for victory. It is never the older politicians in Washington who pay the heavy price— it's the younger infantrymen and their supporting cast. Will we ever learn? I guess not.

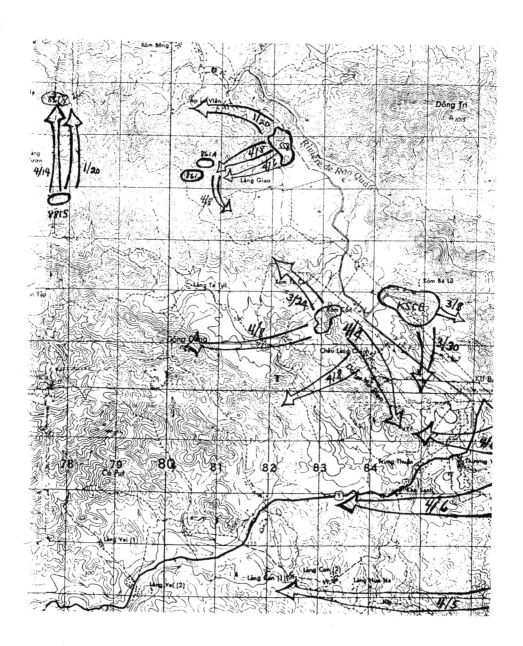

All the offensive action at Khe Sanh
January 20 to April 14

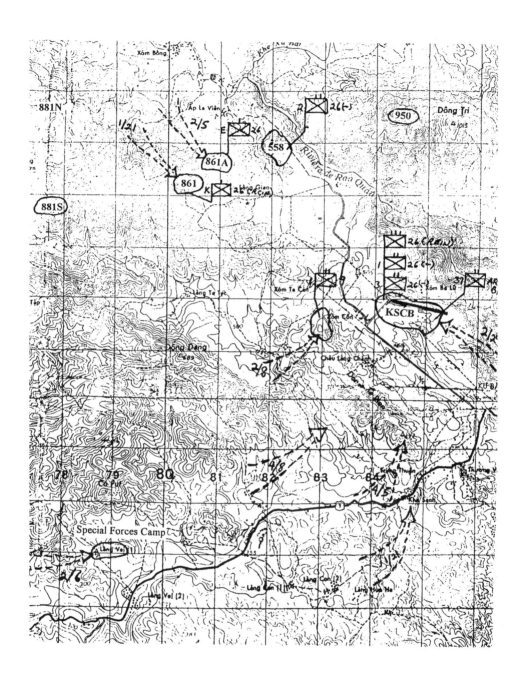

NVA Attacks
January 20 to April 14

Chapter 35

AM I REPORTED DEAD?

EVERY TIME I THINK of this occurrence it conjures up the theme from the book, *The Razor's Edge*. In that story, the principal character comes to the conclusion that life's happenings are a result of "the luck of the draw." If someone had laid out the circumstances surrounding this occurrence prior to my departure from CONUS, I would have been totally convinced I would never see home and family again.

It starts with the announcement of our relief at Khe Sanh. The incoming Battalion Commander and Operations Officer fly into our position prior to the physical relief. They seek a thorough briefing on our situation in an attempt to gather whatever useful information they can. The Operations Officer is Major Bob Kurilich. I know Bob from our days together at Quantico, Virginia. Bob is a good man and very competent Marine officer. It is a treat to see him and visit awhile.

For the briefing I use the terrain relief model I built of the Khe Sanh combat area. I used cardboard from C-ration boxes, glued in layers and covered with green cotton T-shirts to form the terrain. If you cut the cardboard pieces in conjunction with the contour lines on our map and built them up on each other, you get an exact three-dimensional replica of the surrounding terrain. The cotton cloth covering smooths out the surface and makes it look realistic. Any Infantry Commander and Operations Officer needs to be thoroughly familiar with the terrain on which the units will engage the enemy. I point out to Bob that we had moved against the NVA on three separate occasions and that I had walked over three key areas in close proximity to our position. Bob finds the model interesting and useful, but still needs a first-hand look and we both agree that a helicopter reconnaissance will be extremely helpful. After assuming command from Colonel Lownds on April 12, the new 26th Regimental Commander, Colonel Bruce Meyers, also is briefed using this terrain model.

It is important to realize that it doesn't matter what our air activity does — the battle and the war aren't really won until infantrymen occupy the ground and/or destroy the opposing army. This is a lesson politicians just simply will not learn. We recaptured South Korea because the infantrymen moved in and defeated their occupying army. The Israelis won, not because of Israeli air strikes, but because the infantry charged up the Golan Heights. Germany never launched a ground offensive against England and therefore was destined to lose to the English. The Luftwaffe couldn't do the complete job. You can learn so much from history, yet the average young American today (let alone our powerful decision-makers) is "clueless" about world history. I lay the combined blame at the feet of both their parents and the educational system. Despite what they learn in school, they are destined to run into a real world buzz saw if they don't understand world events.

The relief is undertaken the next day. After 92 days (January 17 to April 18) at Khe Sanh, we lift off by chopper for Camp Carroll. As we depart, I look back at the positions we so meticulously prepared, defended, and even called home. It seems ironic that these positions — so important at one time and with so many lives lost taking and defending them — will be abandoned later. I wonder if I will ever see it again; I don't relish the prospect of a second Vietnam tour. I would love to return in peaceful times to these areas in Vietnam where I gave up a year of my life — but, luckily, not my entire life. However, this probably will never happen.

It is about the second day at Camp Carroll when I learn of a message that had reported me as killed in action. Shortly after that news, I learn that the helicopter that the new Battalion Commander and Bob were using to conduct an aerial recon had been shot down. The pilot, copilot, and Bob were killed by NVA ground fire, when the aircraft plunged to the ground and exploded. Unbelievably, the Battalion Commander fell out of the helicopter door! He crashed through some trees and hit the ground. A Marine patrol from their unit retrieved the CO, who had sustained a broken back. While in the hospital, his hair turned completely white!

The temporary confusion on the report is due to our last names — Kur(th) and Kur(ilich) and the fact that he was assuming my billet as the Battalion Operations officer on Hill 558. What would you have thought if someone told you as you left the states that a Marine, a Major, an infantry officer, and operations officer, with a last name beginning with the letters "Kur" would perish in Vietnam. It turns out to be but a flip of the coin, a 50/50 chance, a roll of the dice, or, finally, the "luck of the draw!" I am left alive and Bob is lost. I sincerely ache for the family he left behind and always will remember him in my prayers.

Finally, Khe Sanh is now an officially closed chapter in my life, or is it? This name will appear alongside Tripoli, Belleau Wood, Guadacanal, and Chosin Reservoir on the Marine Corps birthday cakes each November 10. I'm still immensely proud of everyone who served there.

Part III

CAMP CARROLL

CAMP CARROLL

OUR ASSIGNMENT to Camp Carroll is a real change of pace. It is a welcomed respite from living in a hole in the ground and eating C-rations for so long. For most of their days in the Hue/Phu Bai TAOR, the men subsisted on C-rations, carrying meals around on patrol — extra weight. When they did stop to eat, they needed to post sentries so they wouldn't be surprised. Then the move to Khe Sanh meant more and more C-rations. A case of rations consists of about 12 meals. Initially, the troops enjoy some variety, but that wears out fast. They begin trading rations—two mediocre for one good. What constitutes a "good" C-ration? Beans and wieners lead the hit parade followed by beef stew and ham. When all of it slips below good, the troops begin experimenting. One of the best things they come up with is the pineapple jam cooked over the top of the ham in a can. When that wears off, the men focus on the "John Wayne" crackers and cheese, pound cake and chocolate bars. It becomes an effective weight control program that I doubt will be franchised. Toward the end of our Khe Sanh adventure, I can't look at C-rations. Even with first "divvies" it is unappealing. I lose 35 pounds in Vietnam.

To illustrate how bad some of the rations can become, I'll tell you a story that transpired in the Mt. Fuji, Japan training area in 1960. Our unit is conducting field operations and subsisting on C-rations for several days. As we begin a troop movement through the countryside, a poor Japanese woman approaches me and offers a nice red apple for a big can of C-rations. Not having seen fresh fruit for a long time, I promptly reach into my field jacket and make the trade. We haven't moved 50 feet when I decide to bite into the polished apple. I postponed my enjoyment too long. As I bring it to my mouth, a hand grabs my forearm. It is the poor, little old Japanese lady. She grabs the apple, hands me back the C-ration can and says, "Me no like ham and limas." If the starving won't eat some of the stuff — what does that point out?

At least now we are getting hot meals prepared in a mess hall. Absolutely no complaints are lodged against that cook. Even the SOS (s— on shingles) is delectable. The whole experience completely counters our existence at Khe Sanh. You might guess it won't last long!

Major General Raymond Davis has assumed command of the 3rd Marine Division — a Marine officer I greatly respect. He won the Congressional Medal of Honor, the nation's highest decoration, as a Lieutenant Colonel at the Chosin Reservoir in 1950, and, he is a Marine leader I'd follow anywhere. Things are about to change again, and our battalion should be center stage.

Chapter 36

DIRECT FROM WASHINGTON—
MICRO MANAGEMENT

WITHIN ABOUT A WEEK of our move to Camp Carroll, we become involved in patrolling efforts directly to our north just across from Route 9. Other Marine units are in close proximity — the closest being located near the Rock Pile about five miles to our northwest.

One of the larger patrols from another battalion is operating near us in the north and walks into a heavily fortified NVA position. A major firefight ensues. They sustain five or six KIA (killed in action) and are forced to pull back before they can retrieve our dead comrades. A key element in USMC combat operations is never to leave our dead behind. Nightfall comes and they still are unsuccessful in retrieving the fallen men.

That evening we also become involved, since they are making extensive plans to go back, not only to retrieve the bodies, but also to engage the NVA with much more infantry and fire support. Thorough planning takes some time—you don't want to go off halfcocked. That means that all infantry units involved need to be in position and briefed. All artillery and air support need to be laid out and coordinated. These things don't come together without adequate time for planning, especially when the NVA knows you are coming back.

The casualties are sustained sometime in the morning and reported up the chain of command. Notification of next-of-kin occurs the next day. Before the day is out, we receive direct orders via Washington to go back and get the bodies immediately, as several parents have contacted their representatives in Congress. The congressional leaders have intervened with the military command authority. So back we go prematurely — not totally prepared — hoping we can pull it off. The result is a loss of eight or nine more dead Marines. These are unacceptable losses, considering we probably would have avoided some of them if we had been better prepared. This is a clear example of micro-management by the civilian authorities — a hallmark of McNamara's Defense Department leadership. The dilemma of losing live Marines to retrieve dead Marines is simply unresolvable.

I have great sympathy for parents who lose a child, wives who lose their husbands, and children who lose their father. I pray it never happens to our family. However, I wouldn't want to be responsible for forcing a politician to intervene, thereby causing the unnecessary death of someone else's child, spouse and father. Anyone remotely familiar with the U.S. Marine Corps knows we will take care of our own. Our "esprit de corps" and professionalism ensure the job will get done. We never need a one-term representative, or, for that matter, any professional politician dictating tactics or actions on the battlefield!

Chapter 37

GENERAL DAVIS' MOBILE STRIKE FORCE

IT DOESN'T TAKE General Davis long to subscribe to General Patton's attitude about static defensive positions. Victory is never attained by sitting inside a defensive position, such as Troy, Masada, Yorktown, Verdun, the Maginou Line, Gallipoli, the Seigfried Line and, yes, Khe Sanh. He elects to form a Mobile Strike Force of at least regimental size, to reduce the defenses on several static positions (such as Con Thien, A-1, C-1 and C-2), and to be in position to strike the NVA at every opportunity. This will allow him to initiate offensive actions, when deemed appropriate, carrying the battle to the enemy. Audacity — that means to force a conclusion in combat of arms. We will not win the Vietnam War unless we become victorious in several offensive battles.

The U.S. won its independence because of battlefield victories at Trenton, Saratoga, Cowpens and Yorktown. Through swift tactical movements, General Washington carried the battle to Cornwallis at Yorktown and forced Cornwallis' surrender. That victory signaled the end of six years of revolutionary struggle.

It is a sound plan — indeed, a welcomed plan — and we look forward to being an integral part of this potent Marine Mobile Strike Force. I have been waiting to carry the fight to the enemy for some time. Why were we committed to Vietnam if we aren't allowed to win the war?

We await our orders from above with great anticipation. When the operations order finally arrives, I am stunned — it relegates us to the position of stationary defenders once again. The Mobile Strike Force will be formed primarily from elements of the 3rd and 9th Marines, which currently are at Con Thien, A-1, C-1 and C-2. These four positions are manned and defended by two infantry battalions. Our assignment is to relieve these battalions and single-handedly occupy and defend all four positions. Unfortunately, that will spread us mighty thin and incapable of defending any one position against a massive assault.

General Davis is taking a calculated risk. However, this sort of risk is often needed to achieve victory. But this time we are the ones at risk! In addition, both Con Thien and the A-1 positions are just yards away from the DMZ — that is, the line that separates North and South Vietnam. Unbelievable, isn't it?

At this moment I really identify with the characters in an old John Wayne movie entitled *They Were Expendable.* It seems my desire to carry the fight to the NVA has ended with the General's decision. I therefore will look harder for reassignment to another command. If I am fortunate, I might even land a Battalion Commander's job before I leave country. I soon learn that the fates are fickle.

Part IV

CON THIEN ET AL

CON THIEN ET AL

OUR BATTALION is comprised of four rifle companies, which means one rifle company has to occupy Con Thein, A-1, C-1 and C-2. It doesn't take a military genius to determine this course of action. The Headquarters and Headquarters & Service Company will have to locate at Con Thien. Our other units are scattered over a two-mile area to our east and along a three-mile area to our south. We decide to place the headquarters inside two heavily sandbagged bunkers behind the small hill at Con Thien. A helicopter landing area sits right outside the door just below the bunkers. I can't believe we are involved in another static defense setup, and, this time severely undermanned in four key tactical areas. As you already know, both Con Thien and A-1 are located immediately to the south of the DMZ. At least we can stand on the high ground at Con Thien and peer into North Vietnam.

There isn't much we have to do to organize our defenses, as the defensive perimeter already is in place. However, one troubling interlude occurs when we check our northern perimeter. Standing on the front lines, I feel an explosion of dirt on the ground directly in front of my right big toe. A sniper had taken a shot at us. He only has to fire once to get my attention — I clear out in a hurry. A little more elevation on his AK-47 sights and there would have been yet another casualty to call in to the states. This will not be the last bullet meant for me.

At Con Thien we have "heads" (latrines), "water buffaloes" (water tank trailers), electricity, but we are once again on C-rations, and, sadly, no showers. Like most days, we go outside the COC bunker to prepare our delectable C-rations dinners. Today is no exception. I take three metal tent pins to make a stove. After I unwrap the heat tab, I place it in the middle of the triangle, then put our meal on top to heat. We luck out this time as there is still a beans and wieners left. We need to stir the contents in the can or the bottom will burn, changing the entire taste of our gourmet dinner. I set some water aside to heat for coffee after the meal. I always look forward to coffee — it's hard to screw up.

The little sandbag enclave we are sitting in is a little cramped, but convenient to the COC. The walls are about four feet high. When I reach over to stir the C-ration can, a tremendous explosion just on the other side of our four-foot sandbag wall scares the hell out of me — more mortar presents from the NVA. A few more mortars follow in short order, then abruptly stop. As I sit back upright, I realize that if that sandbag wall was not there, we'd both be history. These near misses are beginning to bother me. When will the odds change against us? This is the second time at Con Thien they almost nail me! I further am frustrated because I cannot respond in kind.

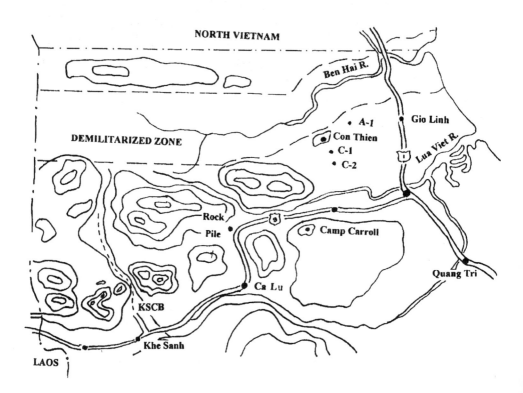

Con Thien Base and home of the 2nd Battalion, 26th Marines. The Combat Operations Center (COC) is on the left with the Battalion commander's bunker on the right.

Chapter 38

AIRBORNE MANAGEMENT

SHORTLY AFTER OUR ARRIVAL at Con Thien, the CO, you and I take a helicopter to visit our company on the A-1 position to ascertain how F Company is deployed. As the helicopter arrives, we run down to the landing zone to board quickly before the NVA lobs a few shells our way. But as we board, they already swing into action. The first mortar round lands fairly close to the chopper. That is enough for the pilot. He jerks up the craft just after the last of our party jumps inside. I look out the open door as we lift off the ground and swing out over Con Thien. Only ten seconds after liftoff, a mortar round slams into the exact spot where we had boarded. We avert disaster by a few ticks of the clock. We head east just below the DMZ over wooded and grassy terrain that represents "no-man's land." Since we don't have too far to go, we fly quite low. Suddenly we find ourselves directly over the top of a large NVA unit that happens to be resting in an open area. We look down and see them scurrying for their weapons. They open fire and hit our aircraft a number of times. One round pierces the skin of the aircraft and strikes the radio operator sitting next to me. He is hit in his lower back and it is a serious wound. They miss our pilot, or we all would have crashed and died — or become prisoners of war — a fate that could end up worse.

Upon landing at A-1 we jump out and direct the pilot to head to the field Medical Unit (MASH) at DongHa. As I step back during their liftoff, I count at least 20 holes in the chopper. I make a quick prayer that the

Major Kurth and Lt. Colonel Frank Heath outside our HQ at Con Thien

young man will make it — he doesn't. When the person next to you is seriously wounded, you obviously feel sick for him, but your final thought is always, "It could have been me." Again — it's "the luck of the draw."

After the chopper departs, Captain Chuck Divelbiss joins us and takes us on a tour of his defensive position. As usual, Chuck has been thorough in his planning and execution. We even decide to walk fairly far forward of our position toward the DMZ to get a better look. I am still on edge about the close call we had and am fighting back pangs of fear. The CO and I must conquer any fear, as the younger men we are leading must never sense we are fearful or uncertain. Fear is contagious. Our chopper returns as we complete our meeting and head back to Con Thien. This time we fly higher and further south of the DMZ.

How I hate helicopters, especially after logging so many hours in them during my Marine career. I haven't forgotten my 1961 crash in one during a training operation in the Philippines. I also had a near crash into the water during night amphibious helicopter assaults off the U.S.S. Tarawa, near Camp Pendleton, California, in 1962. But, most of all, it is those treetop reconnaissance missions down Route 1 that rattle around in my head. Our Marine chopper pilots are unbelievably brave—it takes a special breed to be a chopper pilot. They sure as hell earn their flight pay!

It isn't long before we learn General Davis is on his way via chopper to visit us. When his aircraft arrives and he disembarks, the NVA lob a few more mortar rounds our way. The chopper hastily departs and General Davis ducks into our COC bunker. We are very impressed that the Division Commander visits our forward position. No one ever visited us at Khe Sanh. However, we tell the General that we don't think he should jeopardize his safety just to visit us. He ignores our concerns, but what he doesn't realize is that we don't like being mortared because of a visitor, regardless of who it is! Nevertheless, you have to love hands-on personal leadership. Anyway you look at it, he is a truly inspiring man.

Chapter 39

REINFORCEMENTS ARE COMING

I AM CONVINCED the NVA knows our strength through sheer observation, especially during our initial relief and occupation. If they think we are too weak and ripe for the taking, they will force the issue. We are in a much more vulnerable position along the DMZ at Con Thien than at Khe Sanh. At Khe Sanh we also held a major avenue of approach, but with almost an entire Marine battalion — over 1,000 Marines. However, we barely have 300 men at Con Thien. We also must keep in mind that Con Thien is a strategic position and has been a focal point of attack in the past. The name is well known throughout the world and to be defeated here would be a major political coup for the North. I am deeply concerned about our vulnerability and safety and wrestle with a solution to our dilemma. I still feel somewhat "written off" by higher headquarters. With this in mind, do you have any idea how we might mislead our NVA nemesis? I ponder this problem while dozing off to sleep one night shortly after our arrival. In the late hours of the night I cook up one of my best ruses as an Operations Officer while in Vietnam. If we can pull off this charade, it may change the enemy's evaluation as to our strength and capability.

The basic concept is to mislead the NVA/VC into believing we actually are being reinforced at Con Thien and at C-1 just two miles to our south. A reinforced defense force at Con Thien would be harder to overrun, and a reinforced unit at C-1 means they would be in a better position to defend themselves — or come to our relief.

When I brief the plan to the principals involved, everyone is excited because it is pro-active and deceptive. The plan works like this. We employ three 6 x 6 trucks to conduct troop movements that appear to be reinforcing Con Thien and C-1. We load about 18 Marine infantrymen with weapons and gear onto benches lining each truck. Three truckloads equal 54 men, which is a reinforced platoon. We then drive the three trucks from our southernmost position at C-2, up the road and into C-1. Upon arrival at C-1, we pull the trucks out of sight and leave the benches in the truck beds. The men lie face down in the truck beds covered with tarps. Their equipment is hidden in the cab of the trucks. This way you cannot see the men and our trucks look empty as they race down the road back to C-2. When they arrive at C-2, they pull out of sight and again the men take their upright seating positions. The trucks once more head northward only this time to Con Thien. We repeat the deception at Con Thien and the trucks pull out after "apparently" unloading their cargo. We do this twice so that it appears over 100 Marines are transported to Con Thien as reinforcements. An addition of this size should make a significant impact on the forces opposing us. Just maybe it will give them pause before launching a major assault.

I feel more secure after this deception as I am certain the whole operation was being monitored by the NVA from its nearby observation posts. In fact, it later is confirmed that this is exactly what happened. Months later, in an offensive operation by the Mobile Strike Force, they uncovered a chronicle of our troop movements with notation saying that Con Thien was reinforced! I was proud that this ruse went over so well. It certainly proves that people often see what they expect to see — and that we need to look further to consider all possibilities.

Chapter 40

GENERAL DRAKE'S VISIT

GENERAL DAVIS wasn't the only General officer to visit our position. One day we receive notification that Brigadier General Drake from the 3rd Marine Division Headquarters is inbound for a visit. When General Drake arrives, we move quickly into the COC nestled against Con Thien Hill *(see picture)*. I conduct a fairly quick briefing of our disposition, as there really isn't much to report. He is a tall and rather striking man with a very cordial demeanor. He seems genuinely interested in our activities and our well being. He even asks me outright if there is anything I want or need. You have now been in Vietnam nine months, so what is your reply? Mine is simple, "General, next time you are here bring me a six-pack of beer." His response is "No problem, I can do that." Well, General Drake never returns to Con Thien, nor do I ever see him again in Vietnam. However, as Paul Harvey says, "And now for the rest of the story."

Note: In 1971, three years later, I have occasion to visit Headquarters Marine Corps in Washington D.C. to talk with my Detailer (Assignment Officer) about my next duty station. After Vietnam in October 1968, I am posted as Inspector Instructor of the 24th Marine Regimental Headquarters, USMCR in Kansas City, Missouri. I was angling for the Naval War College in Newport, Rhode Island, since advance schooling is essential for promotion. It also prepares a Major for command above the battalion level.

My old Commanding Officer from Marine Barracks in Kenitra, Morocco, Colonel John Canton, is in the Operations section of HQMC in D.C., and I stop to invite him and his wife, Rosalie, to dinner that evening. He begins to decline since he is expected for a dinner party at his boss' house that evening; and, since it is in the General's home, he isn't in a position to invite me.

Just then the door to his office flies open and in walks a tall, good-looking Marine Major General — you guessed it — General Drake. Colonel Canton stops him to introduce me when the General says, "I know you." I respond, "Yes sir, you do. We first met in the COC at Con Thien back in 1968, and you still owe me a six-pack of beer!" He looks at me, smiles and says something like "By George, that's right. I do. Well, I can make good tonight, as you are invited to my home for our scheduled dinner party." He turns away saying he'd see me that evening and left. Colonel Canton looks dumbfounded, saying, "Well, I guess we get to eat together after all!"

This very graphically points out one of the true benefits of the U.S. Marine Corps. It is small enough — especially among 0302 (Military Occupational Specialty) Infantry Officers — to cross paths several times during a career.

Chapter 41

DON'T HAVE GUTS ENOUGH TO DO THAT AGAIN!

JUST BECAUSE we are locked into a defensive posture doesn't mean we can't be proactive with our patrolling efforts. Patrolling around each of our defensive positions helps to detect enemy activity and keep the NVA at bay. In general, we utilize platoon-sized patrols since we might encounter a fairly large NVA unit. If they decide to come en masse, we would discover their activities a lot earlier. It is hard to disguise larger troop movements. Additionally, we don't let any patrol wander too far so we would be unable to provide support or withdraw if necessary. You will recall that we encountered one of their patrols along the DMZ earlier.

One of the Con Thien patrols in the early part of May returns from its assigned route without enemy contact. The troops always are glad to get back inside our defenses and rejoin their buddies. Several of the positions at Con Thien are large enough to hold a squad of 13 Marines during a mortar attack.

A Marine who has just returned from the patrol walks into one of the bunkers where several of his unit members are located. As he comes through the entrance, a Marine sitting across the room is eating C-rations and happen to have an apple. Suddenly, he puts the apple on top of his head and yells at the new arrival, "Bet you can't knock this off my head." Without hesitation, the Marine draws his K-Bar (combat knife) from its scabbard and throws it at the apple! The knife bounces off the bunker wall with no harm done. Stunned, the Marine still had the nerve (or stupidity) to pick up the knife and lob it back to the thrower. But it doesn't end there.

The apple had fallen off the Marine's head when he jerked as the knife slammed against the sandbag wall. He reaches down, picks up his apple and sets it back on his head saying, "You stupid son-of-a-bitch, I bet you don't have guts enough to do that again!" With little hesitation and a whole lot of encouragement, the "James Bowie" Marine throws the K-Bar again. This time it strikes the other Marine in the forehead, embedding itself in his bony skull.

The "apple" Marine sits in the dimly lighted sandbag bunker, other Marines laughing, cigarette smoke permeating the air, and a knife sticking out of his forehead, yelling, "I can't believe you did that!" Someone calls for a Navy Corpsman, who appears in short order. No real damage is done since the forehead bone is one of the thickest of the human body. When I learn about the casualty, I am required to file a SITREP to higher headquarters. This definitely is not the type of report that is well received by higher authority. When we transmit it, Division HQ calls confirming whether the event actually happened. They think we might be making some feeble attempt at humor! How would you feel telling your boss that the casualty is not combat-related, but rather a "William Tell" knife-throwing incident among your own troops? The whole thing must have sounded like a breakdown of discipline and common sense. Our discipline is actually outstanding, but as for prudence — you be the judge. I guess it proves that you should never challenge a Marine to do anything!

Chapter 42

I CAN'T SEE A DAMN THING IN THIS RAIN

ON ANOTHER COMBAT PATROL conducted out of Con Thien a rather strange drama unfolds. Captain Broughton, H Company Commander with us at Con Thien, organizes and leads a reinforced platoon patrol to the southeast of the base. The day starts partly cloudy, with occasional sunshine and a warm summer breeze. In the area where the patrol is operating, there are many tree lines, hedges and open areas. Therefore, as the patrol traverses this area, the patrol leader needs to ensure his flanks are well protected. An NVA ambush always is lurking around the corner or, more to the point, near the next tree line.

Even though Captain Broughton has deployed his troops in the conventional formation and is prepared, he runs into a buzz saw. The patrol is taken under heavy fire and pinned down near one of the tree lines. Fortunately, he is quick to return fire. He then attemps to consolidate his position and assess the situation. Throughout this action, he keeps us apprised of his situation via radio. Abruptly, the weather changes. Rainsqualls are not unusual in Vietnam, and one has rapidly developed overhead of Captain Broughton's position. It rains very hard, so much so that one can't see more than a few feet in any direction. Under such cover, the skipper begins a troop movement, but his vision is severely impaired. After awhile, he isn't certain where he is on the field! The patrol moves quite a distance when the rain stops just as suddenly as it had started. Clear visibility follows shortly thereafter.

To his utter astonishment, the patrol finds itself directly behind the ambushing NVA soldiers. Captain Broughton, with his 45-caliber pistol drawn, waves it in the air as he orders an assault. They catch the NVA totally by surprise and attack them with devastating results. The Captain dispatches several NVA soldiers all by himself. The Marines, once again, perform flawlessly and chalk up yet another victory for our side.

Battles, large and small, often turn on blind luck. In this situation, Mother Nature's rain provides the screen. If you study the U.S. Naval victory at Midway, in June 1942, it is another case of sheer luck. They end up pouncing on the Japanese carriers from a completely different direction, following their first attack that had totally failed. The Navy dive-bombers streaked from the cover of the blazing sun. In just ten minutes the Japanese fleet was destroyed and the balance of naval power in the Pacific changed dramatically. Although this is no Midway, from our point of view, we welcome a victory of any size.

Chapter 43

CAMP CARROLL HAS FALLEN
AND DONGHA IS UNDER ATTACK

THE SUCCESSION of unusual events pales in comparison to this next situation. I really am "jerked up tight" by this little incident. It nearly scares me to death.

The COC is the combat nerve center of any battalion with both the S-3 Operations Officer and the S-2 Intelligence officer working out of the COC. All communications up and down the chain of command, including fire support, pass through the COC. On any given day, we spend a great deal of time planning, waiting, reacting and fighting the battalion. At Con Thien, I virtually live there, staying up most evenings until 1 or 2 a.m.

The personnel that man the COC on a continuous basis include NCO's from the S-3, S-2, a FAC and several Radio Operators from the Communications Platoon. Two radio operators sit side-by-side monitoring all radio traffic — one handles the traffic up the chain and the other manages the traffic to our subordinate units. These radio nets need to be manned 24 hours a day, so this tedious work is divided into watches. However, personnel assignment and watch hours are the responsibility of the Communication Officer.

One evening in late May around midnight, I am still in the COC doing some planning and waiting for radio traffic to break my vigil. I've never been a smoker, but during those long evenings I carry a lighted cigarette in my hands for something to do, to calm my nerves and to help keep awake.

Things have been quiet when, out of the blue, I notice some activity at the radio operator's desk. Finally, one of the operators leaps to his feet and heads in my direction. He hands me a radio message that reads, "Camp Carroll has fallen into enemy hands. Dong Na is under heavy assault." I spring to my feet with my heart beating like a drum! I remember directing all the personnel in the COC to be on the alert. I ask an NCO to get the Commanding Officer immediately and then head for the radio to get an update and to alert all our units. All the time I think about the imminent assault on Con Thein. If Camp Carroll and Dong Ha are captured, then we are cut off and pose an easy target. I'm sure you realize how perilous this situation is, and you are every bit as surprised and concerned as I am — we are petrified!

The COC quickly comes to life, and the troops undoubtedly are energized to conduct their responsibilities. Then, before we progress any further, the other radio operator jumps up and yells, "Wait a minute, Major, the message is not valid!" I turn to him with a bewildered look and ask him what in the hell he's talking about. He informs me that they both had drafted this bogus situation as though it had come from higher HQ to see how I would react.

Well, I reacted all right. I am livid and tell both of the young men that they are relieved of their duties and to get their asses out of the COC post haste. I then summon the COMM officer for a little chat. When he arrives, I relate the situation and insist that charges be drawn up for disciplinary action — I never want to see those two in the COC again.

This sort of thing is a clear breech of discipline and, for that matter, sound judgment! There is no room for that kind of joking in wartime, as results could be disastrous. It is important to realize that the performance of the majority of the Marines who served with me is exemplary. This incident is part of a real life drama — a weird war. Unacceptable horseplay always occurs in combat, but is rarely reported. You are receiving an in-depth look at the real combat experience. You see — there is no true norm. Unpredictable incidents always occur. Clausewitz in his "Principals of War" calls this the "Fog of War." It's how you deal with these episodes that makes one an effective and successful leader. CEO's, small business owners and military command personnel are basically problem solvers. And, as simple as it may sound, the best problem solvers end up being the most successful leaders — especially when judiciousness flies out the window.

Chapter 44

THE NAVY ARRIVES.
THEY'RE USING CHOPPERS.

JUST AS THE MONTH of June begins, I receive word that a Navy Captain (the same rank as Colonel) is arriving at our position with some secret equipment. We are directed to assist him, when and if necessary. So begins the most intriguing and cryptic incident of my Vietnam tour — it ends up involving a lot of people, including high-ranking officials, and some incredible conclusions. Events like this lend themselves more to fiction than fact.

When the Captain arrives, we set up his equipment in a sandbag bunker near one of the terrain rises facing the DMZ just behind our defensive perimeter. One evening after complete darkness, the Captain sends word he wants to see us. Upon joining him in his bunker, he is standing behind this fancy equipment looking through a lens. Excitedly he calls us over to the aperture and says, "What do you make of those lights to the north?" When I peer through the lens, I see two lights near one another headed south toward the DMZ. I reserve judgment as I watch them move steadily towards the south. What he has been doing with this equipment, he explains, is to bounce a laser beam off these objects without much success. He continues to tell us that this is an experimental piece of equipment that emits a laser beam. Upon contact with a solid object, the beam registers a specific distance.

We continue to watch the lights move at a constant elevation, then drop down abruptly toward the ground. They sit down for a brief spell and then rise again vertically off the ground. Once they achieve their desired altitude, they head north. The Captain turns to us and asks, "What do you think? Well, what would you think? My response comes out without much hesitation, "Captain, those are helicopters, and I believe they are being used to resupply NVA units."

When the "lights" level off heading north, I ask him to let me give the machine a try. The captain obliges, quickly giving me the requisite instructions. When I think that I have the "lights" lined up, I push a button to release the laser beam. I'm not sure how many times I fire the beam, but all of a sudden the machine registers a hit. The yardage meter snaps off a number — 17,500 yards! So they definitely are solid objects and they are obviously enemy aircraft. Their method of maneuvering seems to reveal that they are choppers. Conventional aircraft don't maneuver in a zigzag fashion, and, most assuredly, they do not make 90-degree movements. I obviously rule out UFO's, since I don't think that a superior intelligence would be stupid enough to get entangled in a primitive military conflict on earth. Nonetheless, it sure looks weird!

The "lights" finally disappear farther north, so I return to the COC to initiate a Sit Rep to headquarters. They acknowledge receipt of the message, but I don't hear anything about it the next day. That evening, the Captain calls us over again. This time the CO also accompanies us. When we enter the bunker, the Captain exclaims, "They're back." The two "lights" appear again and head south. Only this time they move much closer to the DMZ and then start downwards. Prior to their landing, I called Dong Ha DASC to ascertain if we have any aircraft operating anywhere near the DMZ. It is my intention to open fire once they are in range. The DASC replies that no friendly aircraft currently are operating in the vicinity of the DMZ.

The "lights" finally land in front of us, but it is hard to determine how far they are from our position. Now, I'm not going to sit idly by while they blatantly operate in our faces, so I turn to Lt. Colonel Heath and request permission to open fire with our 40mm cannons. I believe we should let them know we are vigilant and prepared to blow them away. I give the gunners permission to open fire and do we light up the night! The cannons on a quad 40mm cannon mount alternate fire so it sounds like a drum beating relentlessly. Since every fourth round is a tracer or "illumination" round, they appear to be steady bands of lightning streaming from Con Thein to the DMZ. We sure pump a lot of rounds in their direction.

Once we open fire, we immediately report to higher HQ that we have engaged what we think are enemy helicopters. I even have jumped to the conclusion that they might be Russian helicopters assisting the NVA. We finally order a cease-fire when we see them rise into the sky and head north again beyond our gun's effective range. We have no other weapons that can reach any further so activity ceases for the night.

This time our Sit Rep generates a wave of responses. Higher HQ is excited and tells us to stand by for further instructions. About midday the following day, we receive a message informing us that several General Officers will arrive prior to nightfall to observe this activity for themselves. They show up around sunset for a briefing in our COC bunker. We are very thorough in our presentation, but there isn't that much to report — they will see it all soon enough.

By now it has turned pitch dark, so the whole entourage, which includes four General Officers (one being from the Army of the Republic of Vietnam), move to the Captain's bunker and wait. After some time the two "lights" once again appear on the horizon. This time they move in a more southwesterly direction. They land and take off again heading back north. At this juncture, I feel fully confident that the NVA is using choppers to resupply their troops; yet, I have no way of knowing if they are Russians or NVA choppers flown by Russians. It isn't any great secret that Russian military advisors are assisting North Vietnam. We have over 500,000 U.S. advisors aiding the south for our own objectives!

When the "lights" finally disappear, the Generals huddle in a far corner of the bunker and speak very quietly. As hard as I strain to overhear something, I can't pick up what they are saying. Abruptly they break their huddle, as if they are in the Super Bowl. They move a little closer to us, when one of the Generals finally speaks. He informs us that they are U.S. helicopters operating off the aircraft carriers of the 7th Fleet in the Gulf of Tonkin — to our east! They state emphatically that we are never to engage them in the future. In addition, we are ordered to remain silent about the events.

That's the last conclusion that I expect, but none of us is going to dispute their conclusions or, for that matter, a direct order. They file out of the bunker and into their waiting helicopters. As they disappear, I turn to the CO, Frank Heath, and say, "Can you believe that bullshit!" In the first place, they insult us because they assume we don't know how to read a map! The fleet is too far to the east and way out of chopper range. Also, the aircraft, or "lights," disappear to the north, not to the east. Their ridiculous conclusion only serves to reinforce my contention that something very important is transpiring. This is probably the first report of the NVA utilizing helicopters, and this fact might be an important new development.

The "lights" continue on and off until I depart Con Thien, but we never file another Sit Rep due to our strict orders. I probably will never learn the real story, but I definitely believe it is part of a cover-up. Categorize this in the overflowing "need-to-know" file.

Chapter 45

IF THEY HAVE CHOPPERS,
WE BEST BE PREPARED

REGARDLESS OF WHAT the Generals have concluded, they aren't looking across "no man's land" into the face of the enemy. Unfortunately, they also seem to be dispelling a new NVA capability. We still believe the choppers are there, and when there are two, three or four, there might also be many more. If you share the same hypothesis, then what is your next response? You experienced the whole drama — so do we just blow it off and sit tight, doing nothing to protect ourselves?

An enemy air threat — via chopper — means the composition of an Anti-Air Assault Operation Plan is required. The CO concurs, so I hold a briefing in the COC for the HQ Company Commander, the Rifle Company Commander, and his three Platoon Commanders. It is not a very complicated plan, but certain parameters need to be laid out. The chief issue is sectors of aerial responsibility, and, if you've ever been duck or goose hunting you know exactly what I mean. We divide it up like a big clock 12 to 3, 3 to 6, etc. — we don't want to shoot through our own forces. Finally, when we give the signal to open fire, there will be no random and undisciplined pot shots. It always pays to be completely prepared, even if the eventuality seems remote. The French didn't think German armor would plow though the Ardennes Forest; the Romans never thought Hannibal could cross the Alps; and, finally, the North Koreans were unprepared for Inchon.

A couple of days pass and the helicopter threat takes backseat to the daily patrol routine. June is winding down and things turn quiet — that is, until the helicopter threat reappears! It begins again after dark close to 9:30 or 10 p.m. Someone notices a single light low in the sky headed directly toward ConThien from the north. This time, it crosses the DMZ and you can even hear the far-off drone of the engine. A chopper or choppers seem to be bearing down on us. Maybe only the lead aircraft has its lights on with more flying behind it? Is this an all-out aerial helicopter assault?

Remember that we have an Anti-Air Assault Operation Plan in place with directions to open fire upon the CO's orders. You can see the aircraft now and it is definitely a helicopter. Not only that, it appears it is going to land on Con Thien! The CO never gives the order to open fire since it is only a single chopper. However, the fact that every Marine at Con Thien held fire as the helicopter approaches and lands is a true endorsement of the overall discipline exemplified by our Marines.

By now we recognize it as one of our C-46 helicopters. I personally run to the top of the hill and arrive just as the pilot slides open his window. He yells down that he has a load of news correspondents and wants to know where the hell he just landed. I inform him that he has just flown out of North Vietnam, crossed the DMZ, and came damn near close to being blown away — welcome to ConThein! And, what's more, he managed to land in the middle of our minefield! The window slams shut and I've never witnessed a helicopter go airborne that fast. He pops up twenty feet and darts due south in the general direction of Dong Ha. The troops voice sincere concern for our Air Wing Comrades, but not much for the cargo. I just hope they all realize how much they had tempted fate. Just one misstep by one of our troops and they would have been blown away!

Chapter 46

MAYBE THE DUMBEST THING I'VE EVER DONE

WITH THE TURNING of the calendar to June, we have just completed our ninth full month in this God-forsaken country. Additionally, I just celebrated a heartfelt ninth wedding anniversary on May 30. I am certain no politicians in Washington understand our sacrifice and I still resent their arrogance. The stateside demonstrations against the war do not go unnoticed by us in Vietnam. Obviously, we don't have the whole-hearted civilian support our men had in World War II. Be that as it may, my thoughts turn once again to another assignment. Only three and a half months remain on my tour. I approach Lt. Colonel Heath once more about reassignment, because I am hoping for an Executive Officer's slot with another battalion — time is getting away.

The CO concurs and sends a very nice message on my behalf to the Division G-1. We receive a polite reply, but nothing concrete. That frosts me a little since I feel I have earned a shot. I decide to take the situation into my own hands and confront the Personnel Officer face-to-face. I tell my jeep driver of my plan to drive from Con Thien to Quang Tri, but I assure him that he isn't required or ordered to drive me there. This is strictly voluntary. I guess he wishes to tempt fate too, as he actually volunteers. I feel a little guilty about placing him in danger solely for my benefit. I owe him a debt of gratitude. There is no sense for you to join us for the trek.

We leave early one morning, as it is a 15 or 20-mile drive through contested territory. We pass C-1 and C-2 positions and eventually hit Highway 9, turn east to Dong Ha, then south on Route 1 to Quang Tri. Although we stay relatively close to our positions, we are still fresh bait for the NVA! At any point, we could be ambushed, killed or captured. Placing your life in danger for a new assignment, even if it is a promotion, doesn't compute. This isn't my best decision in Vietnam. Like the knife thrower or the radio operator's prankster, I temporarily lose sight of common sense.

When I walk into the G-1's office, he is surprised both at my arrival and how I got there. Such boldness — this sounds so much better than stupidity — deserves special consideration. I lay my case before him, assuming that there are several Marine Majors lined up wanting my job. He pulls the assignment file from a file cabinet and tells me there isn't anyone currently in the country who covets my job, but he expects new arrivals any day from CONUS. He can't readily find an XO's opening for me, but says he will keep it on the front burner. I can't help thinking that with all the Majors on the Division Staff, someone desires the responsibility of a front-line combat position!

The driver and I once again traverse the gauntlet to rejoin our unit on the DMZ. Upon arrival we look at each other wide-eyed. I convey my sincerest thanks and finally realize that we had just completed one foolhardy trip. That young Marine probably feels pumped that he had rolled the dice with me and won. It makes for wonderful "sea stories" in the squad bay. Despite the stupidity of this action, in about two weeks it actually pays dividends. I am reassigned as the new Executive Officer of Headquarters Battalion, 3rd Marine Division. I soon depart Con Thien and 2/26 with ambivalent feelings. These nine and one-half months together become an indelible part of my life and 2/26 will always be my favorite number. Thanks, guys. And it is now clear my participation in any more offensive ground operations is over. I would have preferred assignment to one of the infantry battalions making up General Davis' Mobile Strike Force.

Part V

QUANG TRI

QUANG TRI

AFTER OUR DEPARTURE five months earlier, the Headquarters of the 3rd Marine Division is moved from Phu Bai to Quang Tri. The TET Offensive has come and gone. Hue City is in our hands again. Khe Sanh is neutralized. And General Davis' Mobile Strike Force is poised to pounce.

My assignment as the Headquarters Battalion Executive Officer may be because it is the only open XO billet, or the experience I had as the Company Commander, Headquarters Company, 1st Marine Regiment at Camp San Mateo, California in 1962. Whatever the reason, I am pleased to be moving up. Little do I know where this will go.

I report to Lt. Colonel Ed Deptula, the Battalion Commander, and hit it off with him from the beginning. I quickly learn that he will be rotating back to the U.S. in three weeks and that a new Commanding Officer will be appointed. The billet calls for a Colonel, and I admit I am curious about who will replace Lt. Colonel Deptula. About a week prior to his departure I learn the answer. He informs me that I will take over as Battalion Commander — I am speechless! What a stroke of luck to become Commanding Officer. I will work hard to deserve the responsibility.

Lt. Colonel Ed Deptula passes the Headquarters Battalion flag to me at the Change of Command parade in early August 1968. Relieving him is a special honor. He was a 2nd Lieutenant in Easy Company, 2nd Battalion, 5th Marines on November 27, 1950, at the Chosin Reservoir. It was here that the 5th Marines turned back waves of attacking Chinese Communist troops. Even though General MacArthur didn't believe China

Lt. Colonel Ed Deptula passing the HQ Battalion, 3rd Marine Division colors to Major Jerry Kurth

would intervene, the Marines learned this the hard way in late November. Lt. Colonel Deptula was wounded and evacuated. My generation of Marines has great admiration and respect for the 1st Marine Division. Their "March to Glory" from Chosin to Hungnam is one of the greatest feats in military history.

Chapter 47

TIME TO WIRE IN BIG TIME

I NO SOONER ASSUME command of Headquarters Battalion when the G-3, 3rd Marine Division, informs me that I also am assigned as Base Defense Coordinator for Quang Tri. For a third time, I begin to organize, or to be more correct reorganize a static base defense system. You should have a good feel for this operation.

The first order of business is a thorough inspection of the existing perimeter and defenses. It takes an entire day of evaluation, and when we finish I am amazed. The defenses are woefully weak, scattered, ill-devised and vulnerable. It is going to take a major (no pun intended) effort to rectify problems and establish a viable defense. The principal ingredient missing is defensive barbed wire, which we need to address quickly.

There are numerous ways barbed wire can be employed in a defensive position. I have worked with all of them. The four or five-foot-high fence with an apron running from the front at 45 degrees is the more effective and permanent type, but no way do we have the time or personnel to erect that system. I decide to gather all the concertina wire I can — there is plenty available because it is the easiest to deploy. Concertina wire comes in rolls about four feet high and the wire deploys as you pull the circled wire apart. Therefore, one Marine can pull the wire roll apart and deploy it on a line for several feet. Each length will then be wire-tied to the other. Four feet isn't high enough, so we have to lay two lines next to each other and then one more length on top of that, making a clover leaf effect about seven feet high.

It doesn't take many people to install this arrangement and we do it at breakneck speed. However, one thorny problem remains. How do we anchor the wire to the ground making the rolls more solid, since they can be pulled apart fairly easily? My Gunnery Sergeant steps forward with a capital idea. We have the U-shaped posts, but hundreds would have to be driven into the ground to be secure. Can you envision how many people performing manual labor with sledgehammers that would take? Gunnery devises what he calls a "flat penis head" iron bit that will fit a jackhammer. The jackhammer is put on the bed of a military 6 x 6 truck where one Marine can drive a post with the pulsating hammer in 15 to 30 seconds! The truck drives down the line of deployment hammering in the posts. Three men deploy the bottom two rolls while two more men deploy the top row. A few more Marines use wire ties and pliers to secure the concertina to the posts.

In three days, we wire in the entire Quang Tri Combat Base. I have never been prouder of my fellow Marines for their ingenuity, perseverance and devotion to duty. The teamwork I encounter throughout my Marine Corps experience is the true hallmark of success enjoyed by our Corps.

Numerous other things need correction or supplement as we prepare a more viable defense. Claymore mines are a chief addition. They are shaped like a crescent moon with the concave side facing inward. The face is a series of small metal balls secured in front of the C-4 plastic explosive. We place many Claymore mines along the key avenues of approach to the perimeter. The detonating wire is run back to a foxhole on the perimeter and attached to a hell box.

An ever-present danger exists as we continue to place these potent and devastating mines. We integrate trip flares into our mining defensive plan. A trip flare has a trip wire strung low across the front of our defensive positions in hopes that an intruder will trip over the wire, thereby setting off the flare. The light from the burning flare allows the Marines manning the defenses to see better in order to engage the target.

On the final day of our efforts one of our own Marines accidentally trips one of the trip flare wires and the flare ignites. Flares burn bright and they burn hot. We look over and immediately notice the flare is only inches away from a Claymore mine! What is our next move? Yell, "Fire in the hole" and hit the deck. We no sooner do that and the Claymore explodes. No one is injured, but it could have been disastrous.

The final items we need to move are the Marine M-48 tanks. Someone has taken a bulldozer and plowed trenches in the ground so the tanks can fit in like a huge pillbox. You know what I have to do! A static defensive position with mobile weapons is even a bigger monument to the stupidity of man. So we pull these tanks out of the trenches and form our own Mobile Reserve Strike Force. We then can use our tanks to engage any enemy penetration of our defenses. Now we feel a little more secure.

Chapter 48

A UNIQUE COUNTER ATTACK FORCE

SINCE THE JOB of organizing the perimeter at Quang Tri is completed to my satisfaction, I set about forming an Infantry Mobile Reserve Strike Force. This Reaction Force will be used to counterattack any penetration along our defensive perimeter. It is imperative to blunt any breach of a defensive position immediately to prevent a total collapse or defeat.

Anyone who is a student of military history recalls the scene in "Gettysburg" when Confederate General Armistead, spearheading General Pickett's famous charge, broke the Federal center briefly only to face the shining bayonets of the 1st Michigan counter attack. The "high tide" of the Confederacy died on the battlefield of Gettysburg. I sure don't want to be the one in command responsible for any disaster involving the 3rd Marine Division Headquarters! I believe you can see the same potential for calamity as you initially survey the situation by my side. There have been several improvements, but there rests still a major concern. We have no cohesive infantry unit to establish our Mobile Reserve Strike Force.

The defensive perimeter is divided like a pie into sectors on a circle. Various support units on the base man each sector. These Marines have been through basic infantry training and have qualified on the rifle ranges, but not much beyond that. A regular infantry unit trains long and hard to develop various skills, like assaults, combat in a built-up area, counter-guerrilla warfare, defensive tactics, etc. Since combat and combat service support units train principally in their specialties, our defense perimeter is a patchwork quilt of troops.

This Mobile Reaction Force therefore needs to be a cohesive, trained, skilled infantry unit. Once again as has occurred so often in our time together, another solution is necessary. Where can we find a cohesive Marine unit that has trained together, knows each other, and that is not performing a combat support role? Then it hits me. I know of a precision unit that performs beautifully and also is available — the 3rd Marine Division Band!

I meet with the bandleader at their billeting area near the center of the Quang Tri Combat Base. As the Headquarters Battalion Commander, they are part of my command. I'm not certain what kind of reception my idea will receive from the bandleader and band members. I am pleasantly surprised when they give me their enthusiastic support. This then will become my Infantry Counter Attack Force. It can be married up with five M-48 tanks, thereby constituting a potent Mobile Reserve Strike Force of approximately platoon size.

We schedule some immediate training drills. Radio contact is established from the COC to the band and the tank platoon. On an alert, the band will fall out in full combat gear adjacent to their billeting area and then be joined by the tanks. I will meet them at the rendezvous site and lead them against any breach in our defensive perimeter. Throughout each practice drill these Marine band members perform both enthusiastically and professionally. Is there anything more inspirational than seeing a military band in full uniform heading down the street in all their splendor, instruments raised, playing a rousing John Philip Sousa march? It's a spine-tingling experience. Now, picture these same band members heading toward you in full combat gear, weapons raised in lieu of instruments, moving in unison with heavy tanks to blunt an enemy attack with sheer determination in their faces. This sight is one that will linger with me for the next 30 years.

If you never served in the Marines Corps, imagine yourself as part of a storied, traditional organization with a 225-year history of outstanding achievement, esprit de corps, camaraderie, and a belief that you can never lose! If you can sense all that, you will understand what membership in the U.S. Marine Corps is all about.

Note: Could this be one of the major voids in the culture of America today? Would we not be better served today if all our youth experienced some semblance of pride in service to country and their fellow men and women? Today, the cults and gangs fill this breach in far too many cases. Foolishly, our pop culture is social engineering us into self-destruction.

My wife and I spend time in Bermuda every year and love it. While we are there, the Bermuda Regiment often conducts a ceremony called "Beat Retreat." Sometimes it is held at night under spotlights in the capitol of Hamilton, whenever the cruise ships are docked. A couple thousand people line Front Street in Hamilton to view the festivities. At a pre-scribed time, trumpeters herald the start of "Beat Treat." The Bermuda Regiment Band, highlighted in spotlights, heads down the street in their bright red jackets playing a stirring march. As they come closer, a rous-ing ovation arises from the crowd. The military band looks spectacular and their splendor captures the audience. However, what they see and feel, I believe, is far different than my sensation. I remember the picture of those Marines of the 3rd Marine Division Band moving in precision toward an objective with proud, dedicated faces. My chest swells as I am caught up in that proud memory that will stay with me forever.

Chapter 49

THE ARMY ARRIVES

AFTER COMPLETING our barbed wire program and constituting the Mobil Reserve Strike Force with the band, the U.S. Army 5th Mechanized Brigade arrives on the base. A fiery Colonel, whom I like immediately, commands the Brigade.

As the Base Defense Coordinator, I know I need to call on him quickly and go to his Headquarters tent to pay respects and brief him on the base defense plan. When I enter his tent I salute, as the Army salutes indoors. He asked me to have a seat so we can discuss how to combine our defenses. We barely start our conversation when a Warrant Officer helicopter pilot interrupts us to report his unit's arrival. He salutes and informs the Brigade CO that he has arrived with five choppers. With those words barely uttered, the Commander jumps to his feet, and, raising his voice with obvious disapproval, states, "Why only five? Damn it! I expected 12. Get your butt out of here, mister, and get me more choppers!" The Colonel's comment is music to me ears. I always have contended that helicopter support is a combat support unit that should be task organized to the Infantry Ground Commander — just as trucks in our Motor Transport Battalion are structured. This, of course, is heresy to a Marine aviator, but I still believe it's a sound tactical concept. There were a number of times in our infantry training exercises at Camp Pendleton and Okinawa when we had to beg for helicopter support and impatiently wait for their arrival.

Army helicopter gunships played a key role in the relief of the Khe Sanh siege in early April. It was impressive to watch them engage the NVA. They looked like a swarm of locusts attacking a cornfield! The choppers were extremely effective and a much-welcomed relief. However, we Marines did not much appreciate the signs the Army displayed on the sides of their gunships announcing themselves as "Saviors of Khe Sanh"!

After resumption of our discussion, the Army CO announces that he is pleased with my changes and progress with the Quang Tri defenses. He also indicates that he is impressed with my experience and assignment as a Battalion CO, since I am a Major and the billet usually is filled by a Lt. Colonel or Colonel. I express my appreciation for those sentiments, especially coming from someone I respect. In the spirit of inter-service cooperation, he cheerfully assumes a large portion of the perimeter defenses. I feel good about this because their infantry capabilities give us the extra protection we need.

Finally, he delights in showing us their new Mobile COC. Based out of a wheeled trailer, it is the state of the art in military planning — very impressive and up-to-date equipment. All the communications, desks, lighting, map boards, etc. are built in and centralized. It resembles General Omar Bradley's COC vehicle in France in the movie *Patton*. For protection, a bulldozer digs a huge trench and another vehicle pulls the rig into the bottom. They then cover it with timbers and earth for protection against mortar attacks.

Note: Eight years later in 1976, I work with another Army Brigade on CINCLANT Fleet Solid Shield training exercises on the East Coast at Fort Gordon, Georgia. This time I am responsible for evaluating the amphibious assault conducted by Marine units from sea and the airborne assault by the Army Brigade. When I visit the Brigade Commander in the field, I once again am treated warmly and see even more awesome equipment. I always enjoy the inter-service experiences because their large-scale operations represent the big picture. These exercises also provide me an opportunity to meet officers from other services. It takes all of us to win — each service dependent on the other in many cases.

Chapter 50

NICE TO SEE YOU AGAIN, GENERAL DAVIS

IN LATE AUGUST a unique event unfolds. I receive word that an Austra-lian entertainment group called the "Kings Cross Review" will perform their musical review at Quang Tri in early September. This is interesting news since no USO entertainment group has ever been allowed that far north in our combat area. Learning that there are several good-looking women included in the show, I know it will be a real hit with the Marines.

We recently have started a Small Unit Rehabilitation Program at Quang Tri that allows a Marine rifle company to come in from the field to rest and refurbish for a week. I think that they will enjoy some profes-sional civilian entertainment as well.

We set up a makeshift stage in the mess hall, since it is our largest building and can accommodate around 400 people. We can reach more men by having several performances. Arrangements are made and the stage literally set.

The day before the show, I draft a message to the Commanding General, Ray Davis, inviting him to attend. I suspect he too can use a lighthearted break. His first response is, "Probably not," but I shoot back a message telling him that the troops would love to see their much-respected leader, in addition to the entertainment. A short while later, I receive confirmation on his plan to attend the performance.

I meet General Davis upon his arrival from Dong Ha just prior to show time and escort him into an already packed mess hall where the men give him a nice ovation. We put him front row center stage. The troops are pleased, since every Marine has a high regard for a Congressional Medal of Honor recipient. In fact, I drank my first beer as an Officer Candidate on November 10, 1958, in Quantico with Lieutenant Colonel Louis Wilson, another Medal of Honor winner at Guam in World War II. He later becomes Commandant. This sort of camaraderie is a real treat for any Marine.

The show is a rousing success — very lively and entertaining. More importantly for the men is that the women are a sight for sore eyes! After the show, I escort the General back to his helicopter for departure. The following week, I receive a personal note from General Davis:

COMMANDING GENERAL
3D MARINE DIVISION (REINFORCED), FLEET MARINE FORCE
FLEET POST OFFICE, SAN FRANCISCO 96602

8 September 1968

Dear Major Kurth:

I would like to express my appreciation for the effort that was made by both you and your men to schedule the afternoon performance of the "Kings Cross Review." I was particularly pleased with both the number of Marines in the audience and the enthusiastic response that was given to the performance.

It was apparent to me, as I am sure it was to the rest of the audience, that the work that went into turning the Headquarters Battalion Mess Hall into a very conducive setting for the show inspired the performers to put on their very best.

Again, thank you for a most delightful afternoon.

Sincerely,

R. G. DAVIS

Major Gerald F. Kurth   R. G. DAVIS
Commanding Officer   Major General, U.S. Marine Corps
Headquarters Battalion
3d Marine Division (Rein), FMF
FPO San Francisco 96602

One more week drags on to departure date. The hope lingers in all "short-timers' " minds that nothing happens this close to the end of our tours. We've made it this far and it would be tragic for anything to happen this late in the game. Yet, we have seen unjust irony happen many times and know anything is possible. The throng embarking the plane at DaNang is loud and happy. As the plane finally lifts off the runway, raucous cheers break out. We gaze down at the people and buildings below, which become ever more diminutive until they blur into a green carpet and finally disappear completely. I can't help but flash back to the day of our arrival in Vietnam when we crowded the airplane windows straining for our first sight of Vietnam. We both wondered then what the next 13 months would have in store. Now we know. Enough is enough. The war is over for us — at least temporarily.

Part VI

THE PACIFIC TRIP HOME:
REFLECTIONS AND CONCLUSIONS

THE PACIFIC TRIP HOME:
REFLECTIONS AND CONCLUSIONS

THE ASIAN COASTLINE fades from view as we climb to 33,000 feet altitude over the Pacific Ocean and head east for the return to CONUS. When our cheers dissipate after lift-off at Da Nang, our thoughts turn inward to other matters — what it will be like to reunite with our loved ones, how they have changed, and how we have been changed by our Vietnam experiences. Many, I am sure, recite prayers of thanks for being alive and reflect on comrades who will not be returning.

Having turned 32 years old in August 1968, this is my tenth trip over the Pacific Ocean. After we are airborne awhile, I begin to try to sort out what my 13 months' service in Vietnam really meant. More importantly, what did I learn?

We share seats side by side on our return flight. After some deep thought and reflection, I turn to you wanting to share my conclusions. I hope you're interested in listening, because I need to talk about them, to get them off my chest, and see if you are in agreement. I decide not to talk at length with others upon my return to the states. The rationale for this conclusion include the following reasons:

- It's over. Put it behind you.
- There are other things more important to talk about with family and friends.
- By 1968, it is an unpopular war anyway.
- There's too much and it will sound self-serving.
- It's on TV.
- I'm not sure I want to be second-guessed or scrutinized.

At any rate, I would like to share with you the things I learned. Since you spent all this time by my side, see if you concur or, at least, see why I advance these conclusions. Here I go:

1. The young Marines with whom I was fortunate to serve and lead are dedicated professionals, ready to perform any mission assigned. They prevailed in battle, supported one another with tenacity, and underwent any hardship without flinching or whining. As General George Patton once said, "God, I'm proud of these men!"

   At its height in 1968, the U.S. Marine Corps had committed in excess of 80,000 Marines to the Vietnam Campaign. The Corps was performing, as usual, in a magnificent fashion. It is so steeped in excellence, honor, valor and history that, at its heart, it feels — no, not strong enough — rather, it knows that success is ultimately assured in any theatre in which we are committed. Those Marine advertisements on television are a good visual commentary on what it means to become a part of the Corps. You *are* changed forever!

   My encounters, worldwide, with officers and men of foreign military service, attest to the high respect the Marine Corps enjoys throughout the world. As an example, my wife and I had a chance to visit the Tuborg Brewery in 1963 in Copenhagen, Denmark, since we were then stationed in Morocco and touring Europe. It was a chance to drink Tuborg *Gold* straight from the vats! I was a Captain sporting the traditional crew-cut, looking like an obvious American military man. Vietnam is heating up! While waiting for a scheduled time to begin a brewery tour with several other people, the door from their executive offices flew open and a gentleman walked across the room. I was somewhat surprised as he looked exactly like the model in all those old Hathaway shirt ads, mustache, et al! He stopped dead in his tracks, stared briefly in our direction, and then came over to us. He asked me if I was an American. I answered, "Yes." He then asked me what I did. When I said I was a Captain in the U.S. Marine Corps, he blurted out, "I knew it!" He introduced himself as one of the Tuborg VP's and began relating his experiences with our Corps as an Officer serving in the 41st Royal Marine Commando in Korea 1950/51. He emphatically stated, "You chaps were magnificent," and then invited

Marta and me on a personally guided tour of the plant. Upon completion of the tour, we ended up at his palatial office where he ordered a tray of all the beers Tuborg brews. I thought there were only three — I was wrong — there are seven! He began popping tops, and we raised our glasses in toasts to the Marine Corps, RMC, Queen, and President, finally ending with toasts to one another. When we left we were in great spirit — in this case, literally!

As you can see, the U.S. Marine Corps is a unique organization and is widely respected. Our country is most fortunate to have such a professional, dedicated and winning elite military organization. To be a member for the last ten years is difficult to describe. The deep-rooted pride and sense of camaraderie that Marines share is rarely found in our society today. All my experiences in Vietnam merely exemplify this storied tradition. We did the job right in Vietnam.

2. The civil authority in the United States never comprehended what a land war in Asia entailed. They were downright arrogant about the commitment of U.S. military forces. Warnings from experienced and professional people went totally unheeded. They are always so cavalier in their deployment of the military to achieve political ends and garner votes. Since the inception of the Department of Defense in 1947, we have not forged any victories.

3. Unlike North Korea, North Vietnam was led by Ho Chi Minh — a nationalistic visionary and dedicated head of state. Educated in Europe, his overwhelming commitment was to the reunification of his country. He successfully took on the French colonialists, defeating them at Dien Bien Phu. Subsequently he won the first Vietnam War and established the independent state of North Vietnam. Unfortunately, we simply did not like the fact that he embraced communism. However, I believe that he did so because of the aid that he would receive in carrying out his goal. The U.S. authorities never counted on or understood Ho Chi Minh's and his followers' commitment. They *were* the revolutionary moral authority for unifying Vietnam. Indeed, they were similar to the leadership in the American Revolution. Instead of trying to win favor or strike an accord with Ho Chi Minh, we were

more concerned with our French allies. We had already paid back the French in World War I and II for their aid in our fight with Colonial England. We, in effect, lost from the very beginning, having never delineated a clear end game. The North Vietnamese attitude was that they would win because of their superior state of mind and patience.

4. Robert McNamara, the Secretary of Defense, prosecuted the war employing quantitative management techniques, just as he applied in managing the Ford Corporation — number of men committed, number of aircraft sorties, body count, and burst radius of bombs became the vernacular. He never ever came close to comprehending the dedication, spirit and camaraderie in the story of the Anabasis by Herodotus (the march of the 10,000 Greeks out of Persia), or the Greeks' action at Thermopylae, or the action at Bunker Hill and Valley Forge, or finally the remarkable performance of the 1st Marine Division at the Chosin Reservoir in Korea. No — McNamara, as well as many of today's leaders, had no feel for the U.S. military, personal dedication, or the lessons of history. He could never comprehend the idea that a 17-year-old North Vietnamese soldier would walk hundreds of miles down the Ho Chi Minh trail with two 82mm mortar rounds. Upon arrival, the mortar gunner would shoot them both at us, and the dedicated young North Vietnamese soldier would be ordered back north for two more! Bottom line profit and numbers were his forte and the American military men and women paid for his narrowness.

We need leaders with foresight and worldliness to lead us in the future; but will voters be smart enough to elect them to office? Civilian leaders should listen carefully to advice from the military and put the country first before their own political ends.

5. The TET Offensive of January-February 1968 was a defining event for us in Vietnam. The VC/NVA came on in force, carrying the battle to the populated areas and on a nationwide scale. In actuality, militarily they played directly into our hands. Out from the shadows, woods and caves they came forcing the issue. And we kicked their butts! They suffered a huge military defeat, losing thousands of their dedicated followers in the commitment. There were practically no defec-

tions by the South Vietnamese populous to their cause. When finally driven out of all their enclaves and defeated at every turn, the North Vietnam leadership had to be stunned! To suffer such a momentous defeat on a roll of the dice must have shaken them to the bone. Indeed, we had won!

Then a unique turn of events developed in CONUS, which turned my stomach. Led by pronouncements from Robert Kennedy stating that we were now losing, and from Clark Clifford (now Secretary of Defense), who had no clue of the events that had just unfolded in Vietnam, President Johnson's policies were challenged. Senator Eugene McCarthy stepped forward as an anti-war candidate and the American youth fell in like lemmings. The college students, armed with inaccurate information, took to the streets, burned ROTC buildings, threatened National Guardsmen, and carried the North Vietnamese flag on college campuses. They professed the immorality of the U.S./Vietnam commitment, but failed to see the incredible immorality and destructive nature of turning against their own military. We were greatly disturbed by their support of the North Vietnamese. Their message to us was that we would have been smarter to flee the country, rather than serve.

The North Vietnamese government witnessed all the civil discontent in the United States and rose like a Phoenix from the ashes of a TET defeat to ultimate victory on the wings of American disenchantment and misinformation. The ultimate result of this development was that of driving of a wedge between those who served and won the battles and the uninformed, naive youth and adults who turned against our military.

The picture of Jane Fonda sitting in the gunner's seat of a North Vietnamese anti-aircraft gun — a gun used to shoot down American pilots, her countrymen — is burned indelibly in the minds of everyone I served with in the U.S. military. Here is a Hollywood star enjoying the fruits of a country that was protected by our military through many dangerous wars. Her safety, in a world fraught with danger, is maintained by our military. If she felt strongly that our commitment needed redressing, it *should* have been done with her political representatives, not with the NVA. To turn on her protectors, to aid and abet the enemy, and to rub our faces in her conspiracy is unforgiving. Such actions are beyond any upbringing and learning I encountered during my entire lifetime.

The TET Offensive was over. Now, the civilian population in the United States was aroused and confronting any authority available. But, what did the average American enlisted Marine serving in Vietnam really think or feel? The assessment by the men of our Infantry Battalion went something like this:

- We denied the VC forces access to numerous populated areas during our time in the Hue/Phu Bai TAOR. Our heavy and continuous patrolling also allowed the South Vietnamese villagers to harvest their rice crops for their own use or for sale in local markets. On many occasions, we gave food, supplies and other donations to the local populace. Numerous times, the Navy Corpsmen who were attached to our units provided medical support for the sick and injured villagers. There were even cases when we took up collections of money for sick individuals, allowing them to obtain more professional help in a local hospital. We existed in austere conditions to bring some semblance of safety to the South Vietnamese villages. Although we knew little of the political background involved, we did know that we needed to serve our country.

- We trudged off to Khe Sanh prepared to withstand any onslaught that the North Vietnamese visited on us. We lived in holes, while still aware of the civil unrest back home. Despite all this, we never faltered in our duties and assigned missions. Yeah, we listened to Senator Fullbright harangue on the radio about our immoral commitment in Vietnam — then we turned him off and executed our jobs to the best of our ability.

    I believe the Marines' commitment was more to themselves, their families, one another and the Marine Corps than any U.S. mission statement. They didn't know the leaders who placed them in danger, but they trusted that they were concerned about their well-being.

6. I'm convinced that the top military brass clearly understood what needed to be done. They either never had the stomach to confront Mr.

Johnson or were ignored. I wasn't privy to the vast amount of military intelligence that must have been funneled upward to high command, but the TET Offensive appeared to be a surprise to everyone in higher headquarters. My commentary on what I thought was a pending move against Hue was probably never corroborated, since they sent four Marine Infantry battalions off to the hinterland. They certainly accommodated the North Vietnamese Military Commander, General Giap. When he unleashed the TET Offensive, five battalions of our best fighting forces were entrenched in the hills near Laos! Had these units been anywhere near Hue/Phu Bai, those areas might not have fallen. It was not lost on the average South Vietnamese village how his fellow countrymen (Viet Cong/North Vietnamese) had captured their villages in the face of 550,000 United States and foreign military personnel! To make matters worse, they also saw our aggressive patrolling activity dry up in December 1967 — what unbelievable timing.

I've given this time frame a great deal of thought and study. The more I put the pieces together, the more I feel General Giap pulled off a major coup on our military planners.

Consider this scenario:

August 13, 1967	Lack of contact around Khe Sanh causes evacuation of elements of 3/26. 1/26 only full battalion left.
September 3, 1967	Remaining elements of 3/26 leave for Quang Tri Province (built-up area).
December 13, 1967	The entire 3/26 returns to Khe Sanh because of increasing enemy activity *(48 days* to TET Offensive)!
December 21, 1967	Marines of 3/26 find "evidence" of enemy buildup around Khe Sanh *(40 days* to TET Offensive).
January 2, 1968	Marines kill five North Vietnamese officers dressed in Marine uniforms near perimeter of Khe Sanh base with intelligence reports "indicating" the arrival of two North Vietnamese Divisions and "maybe" a third *(28 days* to TET Offensive)!
January 16, 1968	Our battalion (2/26) transfers to Khe Sanh, from heart of built-up areas near Hue based on increasing intelligence "input" *(14 days* to TET Offensive).

January 17, 1968	Company B, 3rd Reconnaissance Battalion ambushed near Hill 881N (*13 days* to TET Offensive).
January 19, 1968	Elements of I Company, 3/26 come under fire by "estimated" *25* North Vietnamese troops. Doesn't indicate two North Vietnamese divisions to our battalion (*11 days* to TET Offensive).
January 20, 1968	Both 2/26 and 3/26 launch attacks against the North Vietnamese units north/northwest of 881S/861/558. We catch them off guard and begin kicking butts. We experience no North Vietnamese counterattack, but are ordered behind our own wire. Siege officially underway!
January 20, 1968	Captured North Vietnamese Lieutenant tells 26th Marine Headquarters "an attack is imminent." This causes the break-off of an attack pinning us inside the defensive perimeter. Interesting that the NVA Lieutenant walks voluntarily onto the Khe Sanh Base and is "captured" there (*10 days* to TET Offensive)!
January 21, 1968	North Vietnamese launch a battalion (not a regiment or division) attack on Hill 861. It's repulsed.
January 21, 1968	Khe Sanh Combat Base comes under heavy mortar and artillery attack. North Vietnamese overrun the village of Khe Sanh, except there are *no* Marines defending (*9 days* to TET Offensive).
January 22, 1968	The First Battalion, 9th Marines arrive at Khe Sanh from built-up areas near Hue (*8 days* to TET Offensive)!
January 27, 1968	The 37th Range Battalion, Republic of South Vietnam, arrives at Khe Sanh from built-up areas in Quang Tri (*3 days* to TET Offensive)!
January 30, 1968	TET Offensive begins after all those units move to Khe Sanh!

Then, in order to ensure that we keep those five infantry battalions tied up while they overrun and hold Hue, they initiate the following attacks:

February 5, 1968	North Vietnamese battalion hits Hill 861A. No success.
February 7, 1968	North Vietnamese battalion overruns small Special Forces camp at Lang Vei. They use a few tanks, thereby "alerting" our headquarters to that capability. They never use them again.
February 8, 1968	North Vietnamese battalion partially overruns 1/9 outpost position, but reinforcements drive them off.
February 21, 1968	North Vietnamese company "probes" 37th ARVN RANGER lines, but withdraws.
February 23, 1968	Largest mortar and artillery attack directed against Khe Sanh Combat Base.

After these dates, nothing more threatening occurred. By now they had overrun Hue and succeeded in numerous built-up areas. I came to believe the whole Khe Sanh threat was merely an elaborate strategic ruse, orchestrated beautifully by General Giap. He never intended to engage a reinforced Marine Regiment with our total air superiority in a showdown that he couldn't really win. After all, the majority of his forces were engaged throughout South Vietnam for over a month. He simply didn't have the requisite forces to win at both Khe Sanh and the other areas he hit in Northern I Corps. Also, I'm sure General Giap never lost sight of the performance of the 1st Marine Division at the Chosin Reservoir in 1950 — even nine Chinese Divisions couldn't win!

7. When any nation commits its sons and daughters to war, the leadership must commit to a winning strategy and a final victory. Ho Chi Minh never wavered from his commitment. However, we never understood or even codified ours. That war could have been over in only 30 days if we had done the following:
   • Meet with the Chinese Communists to inform them that we were about to launch an operation against North Vietnam similar to the Inchon landing during the Korean War. However, this time we would leave a 100-mile buffer zone between our forces and their border. The Chinese engaged in the Korean War because Ameri-

can forces reached their borders along the Yalu River. They were not going to allow U.S. or U.N. military forces to camp on their borders, especially after the communists were just consolidating their 1949 win!

- Make it clear that if they did attack our forces again, as in 1950 in Korea, we would use tactical nuclear weapons to defend our forces. If you are going to deploy as an imperial power, our nations needs to act the part. The Chinese fully understood the concept of "saving face."

- Conduct an amphibious landing with the 1st Marine Division just north of Hanoi. Swing west across the north in a large arch pushing south. Simultaneously launch a major attack across the DMZ at the 17th Parallel. If we had done this, we would have pinned them between a hammer and anvil. Does this sound familiar? General Norman Schwartzkauf utilized the same tactic to defeat Iraq.

- Once we win the war, then put someone in charge of the occupation, as we did General McArthur in Japan, to appease the people. Forge a new democratic nation giving Ho Chi Minh a responsible position. Establish a trade foothold, do some rebuilding, and then get the hell out. We did just that in the Philippines, Cuba and Japan. Why don't we ever retain our formula for success?

8. The operations which you witnessed for 13 months made it patently clear that we were *not* going to win the "hearts and minds" of the South Vietnamese. We were indeed viewed as the trespassers! We won the small battles, but we would never commit ourselves to win the war. The South Vietnamese village leaders were caught in a cross fire. On one hand, we were deployed to protect them against their own revolutionary army, the National Liberation Front (Viet Cong). However, we never could fully protect their safety, while the Cong constantly coerced and threatened them. The Viet Cong message was that the French and Americans were foreign western aggressors and should be purged from all of Vietnam and that the country should unite once again. Finally, the VC/NVA were dedicated, committed, disciplined, well-led soldiers, fighting for their cause and their country. You can kill 100 soldiers, kill 1,000, kill 20,000, kill 100,000 and even bomb them from the air, but you cannot destroy an idea.

You must never lose sight of the fact that we live in a nation that does not have the spirit, staying power or will, to commit to foreign interventions for very long. Americans are reactive — never burn Washington, fire on Fort Sumpter, blow up the Maine, pull a sneak attack like Pearl Harbor, or cross a defined parallel in force. If a nation does so, then we unite, especially, when we are attacked or openly threatened by force.

9. The final lesson I learned from my Vietnam experience is that it was changing our country forever. It is the most defining event of the 20th century for American society. We became divided, disillusioned, and mistrustful of government — we lost our moral high ground. *All* through the 19th century we pulled together under the banner of Manifest Destiny. Then in early and mid-20th century, we made the world "safe for democracy." The unbelievable national effort during World War II was something that I'm glad I witnessed. The space race and Camelot were the focus from 1957 to 1964 and then it died in the streets of Dallas — we chose to commit, commit, commit and commit, but not to win. Vietnam remained an open-ended issue for too long.

Now you are privy to my heartfelt feelings. These conclusions are based on my knowledge and Vietnam experience. I'll never know all of your sentiments and conclusions, but I suspect that this experience has given you greater insight into that war than you'll find elsewhere.

Throughout this ordeal, I have liked having you there and talking with you. As we approach Travis Air Force Base and CONUS. I'm about to lose a friend.

When the aircraft finally settles on the runway at Travis and we are safe at home, another tremendous hurrah resounds throughout the aircraft. I've never seen happier people in all my life! Just think, those professional baseball players think winning a World Series Championship is the ultimate excitement. It can't come close to men celebrating their survival and pending return to their homeland and loved ones!

In the terminal, we finally have to face the fact that we are parting company for the rest of our lives. I want to extend thanks for walking with me through this heartfelt journey. A thought flashes through my mind regarding Paul Harvey's, "And now, for the rest of the story." Somehow, I sense that Mr. Harvey would appreciate that you have experienced "the rest of the story!" Good luck and God bless. I wish you success and hope that you will learn even more about history so you can help ensure that our nation avoids making the same mistakes. Finally, may you never forget the sacrifice of your fellow Americans — in Vietnam, in Korea, in the great World Wars. So many paid the ultimate price.

Part VI

THE FINAL FLIGHT HOME

THE FINAL FLIGHT HOME

MY FINAL FLIGHT home departs from Los Angeles, headed for Moline, Illinois, my wife's hometown, where Marta and Chris are waiting upon their earlier return from Morocco. I cannot describe my feeling of excitement adequately, knowing I am only a few hours away from reuniting with my family after 13 long and dangerous months.

As I board the aircraft and walk down the aisle to occupy my assigned seat, I pass a large group of young Marines going home after completing boot camp or on their first leave since joining the U.S. Marine Corps. My Marine green uniform is replete with the insignia of a Major and the ribbons I had been awarded for my Vietnam service. I probably appear as a father figure — I'm certainly feeling a little older! I receive a rousing round of, "Good afternoon, sir!" They look even younger than my comrades in Vietnam. I take my seat and the aircraft lifts off bound for Illinois and my awaiting family.

When we reach cruising altitude, the Captain bids us a greeting as the stewardess starts down the aisle with the drink cart. As she serves the young Marines, they tentatively and softly ask for a Bloody Mary, a beer, a bourbon and coke, or other alcoholic drink. The stewardess, with some hesitation, honors them as men going off to war and serves them all at least one drink without question. The absurdity that men are expected to risk their lives for their country, yet are not considered old enough to drink alcohol or vote is too apparent. When she reaches me and asks for my drink order, the Marines seated nearby turn to look in my direction. I know they are expecting to hear something "manly," like a double martini, manhattan or boilermaker, but instead I request a 7-Up. Their faces register disappointment that this battle-scarred Vietnam veteran ordered such a "sissy" drink! With 15-cent alcoholic drinks in the military, soft drinks and water become just as appealing. Besides, I do not want alcohol to blunt my reunion with my family.

Chapter 51

HOMECOMING — MOLINE, ILLINOIS

AS WE ARRIVE in Moline, Illinois, my nose is pressed to the window to get a first glimpse of my wife and son. Chris is nearly three years old and has changed significantly since I last held him in my arms. I eventually see them standing at the window searching for me. Tears escape my eyes — I can't believe that I finally am home. The government wasted 13 months of our family time and I thank God for answering my most fervent prayer — to survive in one piece and be with my family again! I still pray every Sunday for my fellow comrades who weren't so fortunate and had their lives tragically "snuffed out" for what turns out to be no valid reason or purpose. I will never forget them. I hope you don't either.

Our reunion is tearful and heartfelt. The only glitch is my son calling me "Mom-Dad" — a name that will last for a few more months. After he says it several times, I realize just how hard my absence has been on both of them. Some young children are shy or afraid of their fathers after such a long absence. However, after my wife tells Chris, "This is *your* Daddy," he immediately crawls over me.

The other minor setback surfaces as we climb into a car, which is not ours, but belongs to my wife's sister. When I ask where our car is, Marta responds rather hesitantly, "It's in the police compound. It was towed off the street four days ago and impounded!" It seems she hit a cement barrier while crossing diagonally across a parking lot in the dark — blowing three tires and ruining the rims. She drove as far as she could until she was forced to park the car in front of a store three blocks from the apartment. Since I was going to be home so soon, she decided to save this one for me. Every day she walked to check the car, and, on the third day, it was missing! Frightened that it was stolen, she went into the store to ask if they knew what had happened to it. The store manager confessed that he thought it was an abandoned car and had called the police. She immediately called the police station and explained what had happened and that I would take care of it when I returned to the states. The next day, I pay the impoundment fee and mount new tires and rims. This inconvenience and expense don't upset me. Thirteen months in Vietnam put things in perspective — at least no one is shooting at me! Nothing can dampen my exhilaration about being home.

Chapter 52

TOPEKA VISIT

AS A YOUNGSTER growing up in Wisconsin, I really loved the movies. Hopalong Cassidy, Roy Rogers and Lash LaRue were all heroes of mine. The "good guys" always won and they brought the "bad guys" to justice. During World War II, I was enthralled by the newsreels that ran at the movies just prior to the cartoons and the full-length feature. I saw pictures of Patton racing across France, MacArthur returning to the Philippines, and Marines raising the flag on Iwo Jima. It engendered patriotism and pride. And I celebrated, along with millions of other Americans, during the World War II victory parades held in New York and Washington. They were the good guys! As I studied more history in high school, I came across pictures of other victory parades in Washington following the Spanish-American War and World War I. Too many Americans have forgotten Teddy Roosevelt and his "Rough Riders" or General "Black Jack" Pershing of World War I fame.

I am certain there will be no parades or fanfare when we return from Vietnam or that we will be considered the good guys. After all, the Korean War participants also never received their due. The chasm between those serving in the military in 1950/53 or 1965/68 and the '60s anti-war demonstrators is wider than the rife between the Catholic Church and the 17th century Reformation Movement. This is a good analogy, since the demonstrators actually see themselves as reformers as well. So, despite the lack of fanfare, I still am happy to rejoin my family upon my return — this is fanfare enough!

After a 30-day leave period, during which we visit all our relatives in Wisconsin, Illinois and Missouri, I report to my next duty station. I assume the duties as Inspector-Instructor (Advisor) for the newly formed Headquarters, 24th Marine Regiment (Kansas City, Missouri) of the Reserve, 4th Marine Division — which actually is headquartered in New Orleans. The Division has three regimental headquarters, with the other two located near the San Francisco and Boston areas.

At our first staff meeting in early November 1968, I meet Lt. Colonel Bill Roberts, who is the Reserve Regimental Executive Officer. He also serves as a member of the State of Kansas House of Representatives. The regiment will not have a Commanding Officer, Colonel Al Mackin, until May 1970, so Bill is the senior officer. Over the years 1969-1972, the 24th Marines HQ staff and subordinate units develop into a very proficient unit fully prepared for any military contingency. *(See photo.)*

In early December, Lt. Colonel Roberts invites me to visit him at the State Capitol in Topeka, Kansas, just before the House recesses for the Christmas holiday. It seems several lobbyists are throwing parties all over town. He thinks that I would like to see the House in session, and afterward enjoy the hospitality provided by the oil, tobacco, insurance, farm and other lobbyists. They have their own suite of rooms in one of the local hotels and provide nice food layouts and libations — and it's free!

I jump at the chance. The day before I leave for Topeka, he calls again telling me to wear my Marine Corps green uniform. I protest, explaining that I wanted to enjoy civilian life and not be on display, but he insists. I arrive in Topeka at the Capitol and find the House visitors' gallery, which overlooks the entire chamber. However, I am surprised that I am the sole attendee in the gallery.

I sit in the front row so I can see all the representatives' desks. The place is a hubbub of activity with House members scattered over the chamber floor. Most of them are in small groups engaged in lively discussion. I scan the floor looking for Bill and finally locate him in a small group in the back of the room. After awhile he looks up and sees me as well. Then, abruptly, he breaks away from the other representatives and moves rapidly toward the speaker's chair. The next thing I hear is the speaker's gavel repeatedly striking the wooden base. He calls for all members to return to their seats and takes the floor.

To my surprise, the speaker makes an announcement that will live with me forever. He says, "Members of the Kansas House of Representatives, we are fortunate to have a Marine Corps Major and veteran of Khe Sanh visiting us today. He has just returned from a 13-month tour of duty of Vietnam. Please rise and give him an ovation." With that, the entire House of Representatives of the great State of Kansas rises and begins clapping! My heart beats fast as I struggle to contain my emotion. I wish you could be standing along side me to enjoy this occasion. They continue clapping so I stand up. I do the one thing I know will show my appreciation — I snap off a hand salute to return their respect. When it is over, I think to myself, "I never participated in any victory parade in Washington with thousands of cheering bystanders. But, in actuality, I received personal recognition far greater than that. It is a defining moment in my life and will never be forgotten. I am, finally, the "good guy"!

Pictured: Back row — Captain Higgenbotham, Major Besheer, Captain Axtell, Captain Gott, Colonel Mackin, Captain Johnson, Lt. Groneman, Captain Gallagher (Asst. I&I), Captain Metheny, Major Kurth.
Kneeling: Captain Lindsay, Captain Pritchard, Captain McMasters, Major Huffman (S-3), Lt. Shumate, Lt. Molen, Major Pyle.

The 24th Marine Regiment, 4th Marine Division (Reserve) staff assembled for a photo during a command post exercise in Kansas City, MO. The headquarters was preparing for the entire regiment's participation in "Operation High Desert" during August 1970. This was to be the largest USMC Reserve exercise in the history of the Marine Corps. We were joined at Camp Pendleton, CA, by the 25th Marines from the West Coast. The operation went so well that we received a letter of congratulations from the Assistant Commandant of the Marine Corps, General Raymond Davis, my old 3rd Marine Division Commanding Officer.

8 July 1971

Dear Al,

I would like to convey my personal appreciation to you and Major Kurth for an excellent briefing on the 24th Marines during my Kansas City visit last week. I also wish to extend my congratulations for the contributions of your units to the "High Desert" operation. The reports of your performance were highly commendable

Best wishes to all for continued success.

Sincerely,

R. G. DAVIS
General, U.S. Marine Corps

Colonel F. Mackin, USMCR
Commanding Officer, 24th Marines
FMF USMCR
3100 E. 47th Street
Kansas City, Missouri

Chapter 53

THE TAXMAN COMETH

REMEMBER the Mercedes-Benz I ordered during the Khe Sanh siege? I completely forgot the matter. It has resurrected. Shortly after I report to my new duty station in Kansas City, Missouri, I receive a letter from Germany telling me that one maroon 440 1969 Mercedes-Benz will arrive at Bayonne, New Jersey, in early November 1968. To add to the surprise was notice of the balance of $3,600 due to pay for the vehicle. It is a bargain — a new 1969 four-door Mercedes-Benz for a total of $4,000! Thus I have to fly to New Jersey to collect it. (I will trade it in 1979 for the same amount on an American car.)

In the summer of 1970, a letter arrives at our home with that scary IRS return address. Is there anyone who welcomes correspondence from the IRS? My fears are justified, as this isn't good news. The letter begins by informing me that the IRS is aware I imported a foreign car in 1968 and had failed to pay a Manufacturer's Tax of $700. Since I hadn't paid the tax when it was due, it is not only due immediately but I must pay $700 in penalties. According to our gracious IRS, my bargain luxury car just cost an additional amount of $1,400 — due immediately.

I take great care in drafting my rather lengthy response. When I show it to my wife, she says that we can't send a letter like that to the IRS. However, I feel it is perfect since it is both truthful and heartfelt. I simply tell them that I had completed all the paperwork sent to me while negotiating for the car and I thought the tax portion was included. If they had already sent me correspondence regarding the required tax, it never reached me as some of the aircraft carrying our mail to Khe Sanh were shot down and the mail was irretrievable! Additionally, all my attention was focused on the war and I may have overlooked this little detail. I laid it on thick! Since I was a responsible Marine Corps officer and fellow federal employee, I would never attempt to mislead the IRS. We held little hope of any consideration, yet it was worth a try. You get a lot of no's in life, but once in awhile you get a yes.

About three weeks later, back comes the IRS response. The first sentence went something like this:

Dear Major Kurth:

Your response was most interesting. So, let us get past all the fluff. We will waive the $700 penalty. Just forward the original $700 manufacturer's tax, immediately.

Needless to say, I fulfilled their instructions immediately. With that silly letter, the last vestige of my Vietnam experience ends.

Chapter 54

MEMORY BANK

THE QUESTION BEGS, "Jerry, how can you recall and share in detail all those events over 30 years later?" Well, here I'd like to use a concept that I learned from my son during a recent father-son trip to Mazatlan, Mexico.

While we sit on the beach, Chris hands me a book to read written by the famous psychologist, G.I. Gurdjieff. In this book, Gurdjieff explains why my Vietnam experience is still so vividly etched into my memory. Gurdjieff says, "Consciousness is a particular kind of awareness, awareness of one's self, of who one is. The *highest* moments of consciousness creates memory." In fact, Gurdjieff teaches that man never is consistently conscious of his surroundings, unless he is somehow *forced* into a state of fuller consciousness. And, the more you are conscious, the more you'll remember.

Well, in Vietnam, I was indeed conscious a majority of the time. This was due to my continuing responsibilities, my personal fears and my one-pointed focus on survival. To drift off would have meant increased mistakes and it might have spelled disaster for many. This is why these events have become an unbelievable part of my life. Gurdjieff is right, "Forgetting is the enemy!"

EPILOGUE

HERE WE STAND at the beginning of a new century, 25 years after the last helicopter lifted off the roof of the U.S. Embassy in Saigon, thereby ending our Vietnam commitment. We had lost. The division that erupted throughout our population has grown even wider. And those of us who served in this war feel that the politicians, press and many of our fellow citizens let us down. We were hung out on a limb and they chopped it off. The principal reason I left the military is because I felt used. Indeed, I was observant and intelligent enough to see the handwriting on the wall. Vietnam would become the model for future international deployment and dealings. The politicians would continue to use us for questionable involvements with unknown outcomes.

We had gone through a metamorphosis as a nation. We had burst onto the imperialistic scene with our victory in the Spanish American War. Then we were center stage in two World Wars, stemming both imperialistic dreams and an ideology that we felt was threatening mankind. However, let's always keep in mind that the United States did not voluntarily jump into the Second World War to save England, Europe, the Jews, China or anyone else, for that matter. It was the "surprise" attack at Pearl Harbor that thrust us into the fray. Once involved, our giant industrial capacity and human resolve ensured our victory.

However, by 1947, the world had become sharply divided by the shadow of the *Iron Curtain*. For over 40 years our policy was to stem the Red menace. Korea was the first test, and we jumped in with ground forces forging at least a tie. The Vietnam commitment would follow.

When U.S. forces were committed to yet another undeclared war, the civilian leadership and prosecution of the war by President Johnson and Robert McNamara was flawed. Considering that they refused the military's request to interdict the Ho Chi Minh trail or pursue an air war in the north and allowed sanctuaries in Laos and Cambodia, our chances of winning were negated. Our victories on the battlefield would never lead to an overall victory because the North Vietnamese continued to wage the war, seeing the divisiveness in the U.S. They listened to the world news and took heart at our "civil war." They were encouraged further when notables such as Jane Fonda, Tom Hayden and Ramsey Clark visited Hanoi. A former North Vietnamese Colonel, Bui Tin, who defected to the West after his disillusionment with the communist methods, made Hanoi's strategy very clear when he commented that America's anti-war movement was "essential to our strategy." He further states that had Johnson allowed the U.S. military to block the Ho Chi Minh trail, Hanoi could not have been victorious.

The Vietnam War was not immoral as we were continuing to block the spread of totalitarian communism. This was clearly exposed years later. The true immoralities were North Vietnam's flagrant disregard for the Paris Peace Accords that they signed, the North's final victory in 1975, and their treatment of the South Vietnamese population after our pullout. Thousands were killed and sent to "reeducation camps," and any possibility for representative government disappeared. How graphic were the pictures of the Vietnamese "boat people" drowning at sea while attempting to flee the new communist regime.

The detailed and true accounts of the tyrannical, dictatorial, savage and cruel behavior of the DRV (Democratic Republic of Vietnam) government can be found in sources such as retired Naval Captain Jerry Coffee's book entitled *Beyond Survival*. A prisoner for seven years, he vividly unveils the true nature of North Vietnam. The North's number one goal was to enslave all the people of Vietnam under the banner of communism and gain personal power. No freely elected legislative bodies planned!

Did the liberal anti-war demonstrators believe for one second that their lives would be freer living in a communist regime or that free elections and democratic principles would prevail! Years later any belief that human rights and freedom would reign in a communist state died in Beijing's Tiananmen Square. The communist system proved flawed — then cracked and shattered with the tumbling down of the infamous Berlin Wall.

The leaders of the DRV now are moving to embrace the free-enterprise system in order to advance the living standard of their people. Who leads this economic assault throughout the world, but the good old USA. Had we prevailed and acted as a true mentor for all of Vietnam (as we did in Japan and in Europe with the Marshall Plan), there would have been five economic "tiger" nations today in Southeast Asia (Singapore, Taiwan, Hong Kong, South Korea *and* Vietnam), instead of four.

Just ponder where South Korea would be today if we did not stop the aggression and communist expansion of the North in 1950-53. North Korea is starving, oppressive, lacking individual freedom and still communist. South Korea, however, is not only free and prosperous, but also a key player in Southeast Asia and the world economy. Seoul even hosted the Olympic games. Thousands of prosperous, free and educated South Korean tourists land in Los Angeles weekly. I personally have witnessed a Boeing 747 unload in Los Angeles with hundreds of South Koreans smiling from ear to ear as they cleared customs for their visit. Meanwhile, the North Korean people eke out a daily existence and North Vietnam struggles for an economic renaissance.

The American anti-war demonstrators brought this agony on the people of the South and caused an unresolvable fracture within our own country. It is obvious they were not concerned about the people of Vietnam, only their unwillingness to serve and support their country. Their ultimate goal was to bring down their own nation. They were spoiled, naïve and uninformed. Thank heavens they did not succeed in destroying American democracy in favor of anarchy or "dictatorship of the proletariat," as 20 years later we were celebrating the demise of the communist economy and political system of government.

We all returned to a divided United States unappreciative of our sacrifice. Thus, many turned inward. I personally was horrified at my fellow Americans' support of the very forces I faced eyeball to eyeball. We fought for the survival and acceptance of our comrades — following the legal civil orders — and prayed for nothing more. Then we had to face these unknowing, inexperienced, undisciplined turncoats at home. Our sacrifices faded into oblivion and we quietly went on with our lives. It was evident that our fellow Americans would never comprehend our involvement and sacrifice or know of our victories.

The anti-war demonstrators became our adversaries, setting a dangerous precedent not easily rectified. Will the next generation go passively to another commitment abroad, lacking government fortitude, backing or understanding?

It became obvious to me in the early '70s that if I didn't wish to be used again in some half-ass foreign adventure, I'd better leave the service. That premise was validated by our tragedy in Lebanon, our ignominious departure from Somalia, the Iraq folly, and now the Balkan fiasco. After all, I initially joined and decided to make the Marine Corps my career because I felt it was my duty to defend our freedom. By 1975, my reasoning had changed.

With the advent of the "all volunteer" military in 1971, you have the final barrier erected between service to country expounded by "Camelot" and service by a few volunteers in a "professional army" — a situation greatly feared by George Washington. This is the absolute antithesis of our founding fathers' ideas. The Swiss recognize the dangers of establishing a Praetorian Guard and the importance of a civilian army comprised of all its citizens. Every male is required to serve his country for two weeks every year and to maintain a weapon in his home at all times until retirement. When was their last conflict? Remember, in 1781, the Continental Army advanced the idea that General George Washington become King. Only Washington himself prevented it — berating his comrades for even suggesting such a betrayal of the democratic ideals for which they had fought so hard. Today, the all-volunteer force is substantially underpaid. A large number of enlisted personnel under the grade of E-6 live below the federal poverty level. They subsist on food stamps, local charities and other handouts. The Clinton administration has done nothing about this inequity and yet he has deployed these troops more than any other president — unusual for a man who stated he "loathes" the military. Does anyone else see a very dangerous situation here? We worry about firearms in America and the National Rifleman Association. Let's not forget that our military/government has the majority of weapons — all kinds. In the last century, over 63,000,000 people died in foreign wars, while 131,000,000 were killed by their own governments. You would think by now we would know that you can never fully trust government. The "right to bear arms" is in the Constitution in part as a protection of democracy against a government that could turn into a dictatorship under the right set of circumstances. In my opinion, the formation of an all-voluntary military will eventually lead to the following unfortunate events.

- Failure to instill service to country that President Kennedy alluded to in his famous inaugural speech—"Ask what you can do for your country—not what your country can do for you." It will destroy the citizen soldier—the minuteman, and, with that, the start of the decline of our democratic society. Before he died, Jefferson wrote in a letter to the President of Norwich College that all universities in the United States should offer military training to its students so we would be prepared to defend our way of life.

- An all-volunteer force is basically a Praetorian Guard—a narrow, self-serving institution that could some day slip into a mercenary army and turn on the citizenry. If you tend to dismiss this, then let me suggest that you don't understand cyclical history, cyclical economics, and the role of the "hero" throughout history! Even though a prevailing zeitgeist may determine many events, it still takes visionary leaders to execute the "historic facts."

- The all-volunteer concept is resulting in a continuous decline in the quality of our military competence and readiness. Our military is scrambling to find enough volunteers and lowering acceptance requirements to meet the numbers. Since we do not draft people across the board with a wide range of education, skills, talents and experience, we can't even fully man the sophisticated equipment that we've built.

How can we survive if the elite and wealthy turn against their military? Their children need to participate in the world's greatest political experiment, not turn their backs on it. I take it to heart when I read of John F. Kennedy's PT 109, Harry Truman's World War I service, Sterling Hayden's work in the OSS, Bob Hope's travels to bring the military some comic relief, or Ted Williams giving four years of his baseball prime to fly Marine fighter aircraft in two wars. Ted Williams holds a special place in the memories of all the Marines of my generation. Consider his 1998 comments, "It was the greatest experience of my life, and the greatest people in the world that I ever met were in the Marine Corps." I certainly second that sentiment. It takes character and commitment to "build" a nation, but it also takes character and commitment to "maintain" our way of life. If we continue to get the leadership and demeanor of our current politicians, the day of reckoning will come during my grandson's lifetime.

The American society has settled into an affluent lifestyle, and, in too many instances, with no commitment to anyone but themselves. Many male youths between the ages of 18 and 25, products of broken homes, wander aimlessly and bitterly through our society. They never experience any discipline, or, more importantly, societal involvement. Recall the formation of the "Brown Shirts" in Germany! The riots in Seattle during the IMF (International Monetary Fund) meeting were very unsettling for many people, especially during strong economic times. A deep recession or depression could be the final nail in the coffin. But — just maybe — it could create a new appreciation for our way of life. Like everyone, I hope for the latter, but expect the worse. The danger for an all-volunteer force transforming into a mercenary army exists in times of great political and economic stress. Had those youths been drafted for two years' service to country, they would have become a "member" of a democratic society and felt pride in their commitment. I have encountered countless males and females throughout my life who have categorically stated that their service in the U.S. military gave them the requisite time and discipline to mature and become prepared to enter the real world. It made them better citizens, businessmen, leaders and people.

It appears to me that 1989 was the crowning year. As the Berlin Wall came down, so ended our face-to-face confrontation with communism. We had won. The Red menace was consigned to the history books! With this event, it seemed that our metamorphosis was complete. We were now the predominant power in the world so we decided to put on our policeman's uniform. Since we no longer feared Russian intervention, we started a political process of "selectively" policing the world.

In the late '90s, we had a President committing our military forces at the drop of a hat. First, we attempted to thwart famine and injustice in

Somalia, but then terminated our commitment when United States casualties started piling up and left under the cover of darkness. Secondly, we spearheaded an international force to stop Saddam Hussein and then proceeded to capture half of Iraq, but *not* the perpetrator himself. We intervened in Haiti and the Sudan. Finally, we are attempting to resolve a 600-year-old ethnic and religious problem in the Balkans. Our interpretation of international diplomacy is to press our foreign policy via air strikes against any country perceived as a threat. If politically expedient, we punish nations for failing to fall into line with our particular policy objectives. The British used gunboats in the 19th century. If the Vietnam commitment was considered immoral, then explain the morality of killing civilian women and children via fighter bomber attacks.

For a nation so desperate in its quest for peace, we have now launched preemption and punitive air attacks against Iraq, Pakistan, Sudan, Libya, Serbia and Yugoslavia. The policeman is shooting at the civilian crowd, but we will not send in the Swat Team to rout out the criminals. Our politicians are living in total denial, as are the people, because air strikes have never won a war or altered a strong leader's resolve, much less solved a major political problem. England didn't fold under the Luftwaffe blitz. Germany fought on after devastating aerial assaults, only to surrender when U.S. and Russian ground troops crossed their borders. Lastly, North Vietnam survived massive United States air strikes to ultimately win the war because United States ground forces stayed behind the 17th Parallel.

Then when NATO decides to employ ground troops, it's in a peacekeeping role. Their mission is to stay positioned between the ethnic Albanians and Serbs hoping difficulties finally will be settled. Again, stupid rules of engagement and an impossible mission reminiscent of Vietnam. Albania borders on Koscovo, and (like NorthVietnam) is fully prepared to assist their fellow countrymen into the new millennium! Our newspapers finally are beginning to report the truth with headlines like "Koscovo Chaos Divides Allies" in the March 12, 2000 issue of the *Kansas City Star.*

To demonstrate how political these military adventures are, you just need to consider this statement appearing in the same issue of the *Kansas City Star:* "Administration officials say that an overriding priority is to avoid U.S. casualties and keep Koscovo out of the press in an election year. One administration official . . . said that the driving force behind the policy was to keep it 'off the front page.' " These quotes were on the front page. Do any of you sincerely believe we can win any victory in this quicksand with our current operational plans or policies? I see it as Vietnam revisited.

No, if we are to truly be the world's policeman, we will have to turn the Swat Team (ground forces) loose to ferret out the orchestrating leaders. However, I believe that I know my country's psyche well enough to conclude that calling up the Reserves or a steady stream of body bags back to the United States will not be tolerated for long. Nor will they support a draft to populate the military for continued foreign intervention and policing. Hence, the all-volunteer force will never suffice to complete the many missions needed to correct injustice and brutality and end civil or tribal wars around the world.

I'm fairly certain that you found our experience together in Vietnam interesting, enlightening, educational and unique. You now possess greater insight regarding our Vietnam commitment. Unfortunately, we were wasting our time simply fighting for survival in the Hue/Phu Bai TAOR, Khe Sanh, Con Thien and Quang Tri. The men and women who lost their lives during our eight-year struggle died in vain. This country should never waste its youth in this manner again.

The powerful United States lost the Vietnam War, an almost unthinkable development. However, we were presented another opportunity for a win a few years after our departure. Instead, we exacerbated the situation by placing a trade embargo on all of Vietnam. In so doing, we allowed the Japanese to fill the economic void and begin extensive trading with the Vietnamese. Had we buried the hatchet and allowed our corporate entrepreneurial spirit free reign, the economic benefits to our own economy would have been substantial. We, as a nation, are just too reactive versus proactive.

Since Vietnam, we continue to employ our military advantage as a means of diplomacy. Yet, the U.S. is totally preeminent in the areas of information, business, investment banking/entrepreneurial "know how," pharmaceuticals/bioscience, post-graduate education, and finally farming. Peter Drucker has pointed out our insurmountable leads in these areas on numerous occasions. Why then do we not employ these trump cards in our diplomatic negotiations? Rather than threatening to bomb everyone, why not threaten or imply withholding information, finance, drugs, foodstuffs, and forbid their graduate students entry into our postgraduate programs, as well as send home those students who are now here? These actions are far more humane than raining bombs on the populous or jeopardizing American lives. I hope for such a leader to rise in our midst — Teddy Roosevelt, please come back.

The American press/media could assist our efforts greatly if they would tell the whole story without bias. In so doing, our people could make informed decisions. Edward R. Murrow was my college commencement speaker in 1958 and I have tremendous respect for his professionalism. He should serve as the role model for all those aspiring to a career in journalism. Good newspapers and magazines, TV and radio stations, and other media sources exist and give excellent information. But, in too many cases, the press/media has become the right arm for the liberal agenda in this country, instead of acting as the 4th estate and protecting democracy. Their reporting frequently supports one viewpoint and molds the minds of America. By hearing the same themes repeated continuously, the public eventually incorporates them as gospel. Politicians spin lies into what sounds like truth and only get by doing so with the help of an acquiescent and accomplice press. The media goes after one group with vengeance, yet turns a blind eye towards individuals and groups who agree with its own belief system. Why? — because their agendas are the same. Is there hope for the country when the majority of Americans are effectively brainwashed day after day on one perspective? We need to hear more about *all* sides. A free, unbiased press is critical to democracy.

The only proper and winning strategy in the Vietnam conflict was to target and capture Hanoi—to take out the leader and totally defeat their established army. There was no defined "end game" in Vietnam, Somalia, Iraq and the Balkans. We continue to repeat the same errors — achieving the same results. When will we learn?

INDEX